Nationalism

Nationalism

Peter Alter

A member of the Hodder Headline Group
LONDON • NEW YORK • SYDNEY • AUCKLAND

First published in Great Britain 1989
First published under the title *Nationalismus*
English translation © 1989 by Edward Arnold
Second edition 1994 by Arnold,
a member of the Hodder Headline Group,
338 Euston Road, London NW1 3BH

Co-published in the United States of America by
Oxford University Press Inc.,
198 Madison Avenue, New York, NY 10016.

© 1985 Suhrkamp Verlag Frankfurt am Main

The advice and information in this book are believed to be true and accurate at
the date of going to press, but neither the author nor the publisher can accept any
legal responsibility or liability for any errors or omissions.

British Library Cataloguing in Publication Data
A catalogue record for this book is available from the British Library

Library of Congress Cataloging-in-Publication Data
A catalog record for this book is available from the Library of Congress

ISBN 0 340 60061 6

6 7 8 9 10

Typeset by Colset Private Limited, Singapore
Printed and bound in Great Britain by
J W Arrowsmith Ltd, Bristol

Contents

Preface

In the early 1950s, traffic barriers on the Franco-German border were removed by young Europeans. They were excited by the idea that Europe had embarked on a journey towards political integration. They believed their action to symbolize the ultimate downfall of nationalism as a political ideology that poisoned the social life of man. Anything that even vaguely smacked of nationalism had forfeited every last grain of respect in a continent where, in the immediate post-war period, people far and wide were still demoralized and suffering the effects of material destruction. This was particularly true of Germans. Yet optimism and euphoria managed to shine through. There was a feeling in the air that in a (Western) Europe on the road to economic and political unity, the nation and the nation-state, two concepts that had been at the heart of political thought and action since the nineteenth century, would fortunately soon belong to the past.

European dreams that at least a large part of the continent would rapidly achieve political unity proved all too quickly to be illusions, however. The hope cherished elsewhere, fired by the creation of the United Nations in San Francisco in June 1945, that the idea of 'one world' would soon become reality, was equally short lived. Only a few years had passed since National Socialism's regime of terror over Europe and the unprecedented horrors of the Second World War, and already nationalism was flourishing again, not only in the newly independent African and Asian states, but in Western Europe too. Here, nobody could deny that national – and nationalist – motivations and categories of thought were seeping back into politics, despite politicians' assurances to the contrary.

Today, almost fifty years after the Second World War, the nation and the nation-state have returned with a vengeance. After the collapse of communism it is realistic to assume that nationalism will continue to be a universal historical principle decisively structuring international relations and the domestic order of states well into the next century. To conceive of nationalism as a political aberration, or as an inevitable but ultimately transitory historical phenomenon is to disregard its unabated impact upon politics. Though we might justifiably abhor its extreme forms, we cannot conveniently forget it as a pathological manifestation in the history of modern societies, nor dismiss treatment of its historical impact as irrelevant. It would be naive and thoroughly irresponsible to ignore the blatant dangers that nationalism and nationalist thinking undeniably pose for societies in the age of industrialism, and indeed for global peace. This alone makes it more necessary than ever to arrive at a clear understanding of nationalism, its roots and the political and social problems related to it.

This is a major conviction underlying the present volume. It seeks to examine nationalism as a generic political and historical phenomenon that is manifested in specific, often temporary and spatially limited forms. They include nationalism in nineteenth-century as well as in inter-war Europe, German nationalism during the war of liberation against Napoleon, in Imperial Germany after 1871 and in the Third Reich, and nationalism in the developing world and post-1989 Europe. In view of the vast amount of historical research already done on the matter at hand, such a comprehensive approach adopted here does not make it easy to build the desirable bridge between the particular and the general. However, even though the very polymorphism of nationalism presents problems for a synoptic account of the phenomenon and its history since the French Revolution, it is possible to draw some general conclusions about the social and political conditions underlying its various forms. My evidence is taken from existing works and comparative analyses of national movements and nationalist thought, a whole range of which have appeared particularly since the Second World War in reaction to fatal political developments in the 1920s and 1930s.

Using the available body of research as a starting point, this book considers questions relevant to both the intellectual and social history of nationalism. Nationalism is here understood as a political force that has brought itself to bear in the most varied historical contexts and in a whole number of ways over the last two centuries. In particular the focus will be on the changing political and social functions nationalism has assumed over the years. Logically, this prompts the vital question of whether nationalism, after all, might be devoid of a function in the contemporary world. This question is bound up with the hope that, at least in the advanced Western democracies, awareness of nationalism's roots and history will obviate its more extreme varieties.

This book was first published in German. This second English edition has been thoroughly revised in the light of recent events, particularly in Eastern and South-Eastern Europe. It would have been impossible to write on the subject without the benefit of the excellent working environments of the German Historical Institute in London and the History Department of the University of Cologne. I am very grateful to both.

London   Peter Alter
November 1993

1

What is Nationalism?

I Problems of Definition

Nationalism is a political force which has been more important in shaping the history of Europe and the world over the last two centuries than the ideas of freedom and parliamentary democracy or, let alone, of communism. The roots of modern nationalism are to be found in late eighteenth-century Western Europe and North America. From there it subsequently spread to the whole of Europe and eventually to all parts of the world. Alongside socialism, it was one of the two 'main currents of thought of the nineteenth century' (thus the German historian Friedrich Meinecke). In the twentieth century, nationalism has had unparalleled successes, its importance growing by leaps and bounds in Europe directly before and after the First World War, and then, particularly after the Second World War, in Asia and Africa.

The plethora of phenomena which may be subsumed under the term 'nationalism' suggests that it is one of the most ambiguous concepts in the present-day vocabulary of political and analytical thought. The programme of an insurgent movement in the Balkans in the nineteenth century or in Africa in the twentieth, just to give two examples, may as easily be classified under the category of nationalism as may the oppression of one people by another. It has been – and continues to be – part of the make-up of both imperialism and anti-imperialism. It can be associated with forces striving for political, social, economic and cultural emancipation, as well as with those whose goal is oppression.

In the nineteenth and twentieth centuries, large multinational states which had emerged during the course of history, such as the Ottoman or Habsburg Empires, were split asunder in the name of nationalism, and were succeeded by a large number of small separate states. In the last century and a half, new states such as Greece, Italy, the German Reich, Ireland and Poland were proclaimed in the name of nationalism. Nationalist interests were among the driving forces behind the colonial expansion of the European powers as they created overseas empires in Asia, Africa and other parts of the globe. Between 1918 and 1945, nationalism became synonymous with intolerance, inhumanity and violence. Wars were fought and heinous crimes perpetrated in its name. It inspired the violent expulsion of people from their homelands, and justified campaigns of territorial conquest. For individuals and whole peoples alike, nationalism signalled danger, restrictions on liberty, and not infrequently a threat to their very survival. The policies of extermination pursued by the National Socialists during the Second World War are the most horrifying examples. And yet at the same time, nationalism could just as often engender hopes for a free and just social order; indeed for many it equated with liberation from political, economic and social discrimination.

It is clear that nationalism, so convenient a label and justification for many developments, conceals within itself extreme opposites and contradictions. It can mean emancipation, and it can mean oppression: nationalism, it seems, is a repository of dangers as well as opportunities. It has so many different forms and 'national' variations in space and time that it is often argued whether they can all be accommodated under the one roof. Only with reference to a concrete historical context can we say what the term actually does or should signify. An initial conclusion could run like this: *nationalism* does not exist as such, but a multitude of manifestations of nationalism do. In other words, it is more appropriate to speak of *nationalisms* in the plural than of *nationalism* in the singular. This still leaves the issue of whether the various nationalisms the world has witnessed since the late eighteenth century nevertheless possess common formal and substantial structures, and whether they can be traced back to comparable historical geneses.

Current linguistic usage defines 'nationalists' as people whose action or reasoning gives indiscriminate precedence to the interests of one nation (usually their own) over those of other nations, and who are prepared to disregard those others for the sacrosanct honour of their own nation. A modern German encyclopedia defines nationalism as an 'exaggerated and intolerant form of thought in relation to a nation'.[1] This is a clear hint that, in modern usage, nationalism has negative connotations, suggesting an extreme ideology, and is judged in more or less moral terms. The term 'nationalism' is used to brand forms of collective yearning and aggression arrogantly posturing in the name of a nation. By contrast, the pursuit of 'the national interest' and 'a sense of national pride' are wholly laudable, since they are felt to refer to clearly legitimate concerns which do not inevitably conflict with the nationalism or the interests of other peoples. The underlying idea in this case is that equality exists between various nationalisms, and their frequently competing claims can be settled through peaceful compromise.

As a way of avoiding the pejoratively applied term 'nationalism', the older word 'patriotism' – love of one's homeland or country – is used. In eighteenth-century Europe it bore the notion of an emotional attachment to a city, a landscape, a dynastic state or a ruler. In 1736, the English statesman Lord Bolingbroke wrote: 'Neither Montaigne ..., nor Des Cartes ..., nor Newton ... felt more intellectual joy than he feels who is a real patriot, who bends all the force of his understanding, and directs all his thoughts and actions, to the good of his

---

[1] *Großer Brockhaus*, 16th ed., Wiesbaden 1955, entry 'Nationalism'.

country.'[2] A love of one's country was combined with universal human ideals; it was easy to be both a patriot and a citizen of the world. In 1797, the German poet Novalis declared: 'German nature is cosmopolitanism mixed with the strongest individuality.'[3] Then from the nineteenth century onwards, the meaning of patriotism shifted to allegiance to the nation and the nation-state, and came to be synonymous with nationalism and national consciousness, though in fact it was more and more rarely used as such. Later it resurfaced as a contrast to nationalism, which by now was increasingly being associated with expansionism. As the Dutch historian Johan Huizinga once put it, patriotism now referred to 'the will to maintain and defend what is one's own and cherished'.[4] Unlike nationalism, patriotism has virtually never had the effect of an aggressive political force. For this reason, the historian Hans Kohn, who together with Carlton Hayes can be regarded as the doyen of the modern study of nationalism, has justifiably called it a 'purely vegetative group feeling'.[5]

The term 'nationalism', whose earliest mention can be found in a work of 1774 by the German philosopher Johann Gottfried Herder, did not begin to enter into general linguistic usage until the mid-nineteenth century.[6] But today arguments still rage over what nationalism really is. Even the academic world, which has been studying nationalism for decades, has failed to agree on a generally acceptable definition. The same is true of the concepts of 'nation' and 'nationality'. In essence, the range of definitions that have been offered merely reflects the multiformity that nationalism has assumed in historical and political reality since the late eighteenth century. Since new hybrids of nationalism are constantly being thrown up in words and deeds, in the definition and study of the phenomenon the depth of the student's experience continues to be equally important as the weight he or she gives to the components that, by rather general consensus, must be present in any given nationalism. These common structural components, or features, of nationalism include: consciousness of the uniqueness or peculiarity of a group of people, particularly with respect to their ethnic, linguistic or religious homogeneity; emphasizing of shared socio-cultural attitudes and historical memories; a sense of common mission; disrespect for and animosity towards other peoples (racism, xenophobia, anti-Semitism).

The American political scientist Karl W. Deutsch, whose seminal work has enriched research into nationalism to an extraordinary degree since the

---

[2] Lord Bolingbroke, 'A Letter on the Spirit of Patriotism', in: *The Works of Lord Bolingbroke*, vol. 2, London 1844 (reprint 1967), p. 360.

[3] Quoted in: Friedrich Meinecke, *Cosmopolitanism and the National State*, Princeton (NJ) 1970, p. 55.

[4] Johan Huizinga, *Men and Ideas. Essays on History, the Middle Ages, the Renaissance*, New York 1959, p. 97.

[5] Hans Kohn, *The Idea of Nationalism. A Study in its Origins and Background*, New York 1961, p. 120.

[6] Boyd C. Shafer, *Faces of Nationalism. New Realities and Old Myths*, New York 1972, p. 16. Aira Kemiläinen, *Nationalism. Problems Concerning the Word, the Concept, and Classification*, Jyvaskyla 1964. Eugene Kamenka (ed.), *Nationalism. The Nature and Evolution of an Idea*, London 1976.

1950s, has consequently defined nationalism as 'a state of mind which gives "national" messages, memories, and images a preferred status in social communication and a greater weight in the making of decisions'. In Deutsch's opinion, a nationalist devotes greater attention to those messages which 'carry specific symbols of nationality, or which originate from a specific national source, or which are couched in a specific national code of language or culture'.[7] This definition, which emphasizes intensive social communication as the pre-condition for feelings of national identity, is not entirely watertight, however, for it considers only some, albeit important, aspects of nationalism.

A definition must necessarily be more comprehensive if it hopes to cater for all the forms of nationalism the nineteenth and twentieth centuries have witnessed: the nationalism of peoples which possess a state, and the nationalism of those which do not. The Bohemian-born sociologist and historian Eugen Lemberg comes a great deal nearer to the mark. In the framework of a 'sociological theory of nationalism',[8] he characterizes nationalism as a 'system of ideas, values and norms, an image of the world and society' which makes a 'large social group aware of where it belongs and invests this sense of belonging with a particular value. In other words, it integrates the group and demarcates its environment'.[9] Lemberg goes on to list the nuclei around which the group's awareness of its own location can crystallize: 'shared language, origins, character and culture, or common subordination to a given state power'.[10]

Lemberg's definition of nationalism as an ideology capable of integrating large social groups has been refined by the historian Theodor Schieder, who holds nationalism to be a *specific* integrative ideology which 'always makes reference to a "nation" in one sense or another, and not *merely* to a social or religious type of group'.[11] This broad conception will be adopted here: nationalism, such as it has appeared since the American and French Revolutions, will be understood as both an ideology and a political movement which holds the nation and the sovereign nation-state to be crucial indwelling values, and which manages to mobilize the political will of a people or a large section of a population. Nationalism is hence taken to be a largely dynamic principle capable of engendering hopes, emotions and action; it is a vehicle for activating human beings and creating political solidarity amongst them for the purposes of achieving a common goal.

In accordance with this definition, nationalism exists whenever individuals feel they belong primarily to the nation, and whenever affective attachment and loyalty to that nation override all other attachments and loyalties. It is not status group, nor religious conviction, nor a dynasty

---

[7] Karl W. Deutsch, 'Nation and World', in: Ithiel de Sola Pool (ed.), *Contemporary Political Science: Toward Empirical Theory*, New York 1967, p. 208.

[8] Eugen Lemberg, *Nationalismus*, Reinbek 1964, vol. 2, p. 16.

[9] *Ibid.*, p. 52.

[10] *Ibid.*

[11] Theodor Schieder, 'Probleme der Nationalismusforschung', in: *idem*/Peter Burian (eds), *Sozialstruktur und Organisation europäischer Nationalbewegungen*, Munich 1971, p. 11.

or a particularistic state, nor a physical landscape, nor genealogical roots, not even social class which determine the supra-individual frame of reference; the tenet of Enlightenment philosophy – that the individual is principally a member of the human race and thus a citizen of the world – no longer holds: individuals perceive themselves, rather, as members of a particular nation. They identify with its historical and cultural heritage and with the form of its political life. The nation (or the nation-state) represents the site where life is led, and endows the individual's existence with meaning both in the present and the future. The way in which this multifaceted and subtle process of intellectual transition from the humanitarian universalism of the Enlightenment to attachment to the nation and the nation-state affected Germany has been lucidly portrayed in Friedrich Meinecke's famous and influential study, *Cosmopolitanism and the National State*.[12]

2 The Nation as Central Value

In nationalism, the nation is placed upon the highest pedestal; its value resides in its capacity as the sole, binding agency of meaning and justification. Nations can to a certain extent be regarded as the building blocks of humanity in an industrializing world. National interests provide the yardsticks of political thought and action. As early research highlighted, this often has the radical consequence of transforming nationalism into a substitute religion. The American historian Carlton Hayes has been the most prominent student of the subject to draw attention to the fact that almost all historical instances of nationalism have been interwoven with religious predicates.[13] The nation is consecrated, it is ultimately a holy entity. Service, even death, for the sake of the nation's cohesion, self-assertion and glory are elevated by national rhetoric to the level of sacrifice and martyrdom. National awakening in early nineteenth-century Germany, and later in other countries, was experienced as rites of intoxication and solidarity shared by an entire community. In nationalism, the religious is secularized, and the national sanctified.

It would however be misleading to imply a simple linear relationship between nationalism and religion by arguing that the former gains a hold over a social group as the latter wanes. The Irish, Welsh, Basque, Polish and Slovak cases suffice to render that kind of approach quite untenable, for in these instances religious belief has lost none of its sway over the people even though nationalism has flourished, with the clergy fervently supporting the national movement, and often playing a leading role in its organization and agitation.

---

[12] Friedrich Meinecke, *Cosmopolitanism and the National State*, Princeton (NJ) 1970 (the German edition was first published in 1907).

[13] C. J. H. Hayes, 'Nationalism as a Religion', in: *idem, Essays on Nationalism*, New York 1926, reprint 1966. *Idem, Nationalism. A Religion*, New York 1960. See also Eric J. Hobsbawm, 'Mass-Producing Traditions: Europe, 1870–1914, in: *idem*/Terence Ranger (eds), *The Invention of Tradition*, Cambridge 1983, pp. 263–307.

Everything we have said so far rests upon an abstract premise of the nation. But what should we actually understand by 'nation'? What characterizes a nation? How is it different from a people? Even a cursory examination of the relevant literature suffices to show that, as in the case of nationalism, the number of definitions is enormous, and none has been accepted as a generally valid concept. The most elementary answer to the question would be this: the nation is a politically mobilized people. Using his key notion of social communication once again, Karl Deutsch conceives of a people as a body of individuals who 'can communicate quickly and effectively with each other over long distances and about a variety of themes and matters'. This ability to communicate usually presupposes a common language, religion and culture, a 'heritage of common meanings and memories'. A communication society is based largely on a cultural community. If a people thus defined also possesses its own state apparatus, and wields autonomous political power, then, according to Deutsch, it can be regarded as a nation. A nation, for him, is a people in possession of a state.[14]

There is no need to explain at length why this is a highly restrictive as well as demanding definition of the nation. It implies that a people which has yet to gain its own independent state cannot be called a nation. Yet it is frequently the case that a nation-state is the outcome of a national movement: there is no doubt that Germans regarded themselves collectively as a nation in the late eighteenth century, though a united German state was not established until 1871. Likewise, even though nineteenth-century Poles lived divided in three separate multinational empires – Russia, the Habsburg Empire and Prussia/Germany – they nevertheless constituted a nation. They did not gain their own Polish nation-state until 1918. Deutsch's definition also fails to take account of concrete historical evidence of peoples whose nationhood has not been disputed since the nineteenth century but have none the less failed to acquire their own states: Scots, Tamils, Sikhs, Tibetans, Kurds, and Basques, for instance. A further implication of his definition is that the number of existing states equals the number of nations. This is of course wholly inaccurate, even if for a time the American President Woodrow Wilson, who argued that the principle of self-determination should be rigidly applied, toyed with the idea that every nation could be more or less guaranteed the right to establish its own state. In brief, we can conclude from this and similar examples that a nation may certainly exist without its own state, and also a state without a unified nation. Where the definition of nation is concerned, the actual possession or otherwise of autonomous state power is a rather secondary consideration. Not so – and this is most important – in the case of nationalism as an ideology.

For the sociologist Max Weber, the term nation suggests in the first instance that 'it is proper to expect from certain groups a specific sentiment of solidarity in the face of other groups'.[15] On the face of it, this is a very vague formulation which can just as easily apply to religious communities,

---

[14] Deutsch, 'Nation and World', p. 207.

[15] Max Weber, *Economy and Society. An Outline of Interpretive Sociology*, ed. by Guenther Roth and Claus Wittich, Berkeley (Calif.) 1978, p. 922.

trade unions, professional associations or political parties. But the key word in Weber's definition is the adjective 'specific'. The sense of national solidarity revolves around, and is aroused and sustained by, particular factors, mainly those which we have described as constituting the make-up of a modern nation: language, culture, historical consciousness, mores, social communication, religion and political goals. The significance of each as an instrument of promoting national identity and demarcation from other national entities varies from case to case. Right up until the nineteenth century it was mainly orthodox Christianity which defined Greeks and Serbs, for instance, as social groups distinct from Islamic Turks and Bosnians, despite centuries of symbiosis. When a resettlement took place between Turks and Greeks in Asia Minor in 1923, the criterion used to determine an individual's nationality was, not language, nor the will or personal preference of that individual, but simply religious conviction. In Ireland, Roman Catholicism has been paramount in dividing the large majority of Irish from the indigenous Protestant Anglo-Irish ascendancy and from the English as demonstrated especially by nineteenth-century Anglo-Irish history. But in many other cases – particularly in Eastern Europe – language was a more powerful medium of division and separation than religion or denomination. Relevant examples are the relations between Poles and Germans in Upper Silesia and the provinces of West and East Prussia, between Czechs and Germans in Bohemia, and between Finns and Swedes in Russian Finland.

Common language has been known to bridge even religious differences: this was true of Islamic, Greek Orthodox and Roman Catholic Albanians in the Ottoman Empire, and, at least for a limited time, of orthodox Serbs and Roman Catholic Croats. Language has also been the decisive factor in the Romanians' sense of belonging together as a nation. Obviously, the unifying, or divisive, power of language is brought out all the more sharply where encounters between people speaking different tongues demonstrate the fundamental consequences of mutual comprehension or miscomprehension. This was almost part of everyday life in multinational dynastic polities such as the Russian, Ottoman and Habsburg Empires.

In some cases – Poles in Tsarist Russia, or early nineteenth-century Walloons, Flemings and Dutch, when in 1830–31 the United Netherlands split into the Kingdom of the Netherlands and the Kingdom of Belgium – religion and language together have been the foundations of national consciousness and the nation. On the basis of this sort of historical evidence, the subsequent Soviet dictator Joseph Stalin believed it was possible to define the nation in terms of what he regarded as objective, scientific criteria. In his famous and widely read work, *Marxism and the National Question*, which he wrote early in 1913, obviously at Lenin's behest, Stalin describes the nation as a 'historically evolved, stable community'. It is characterized by four main features: it was a community of language, of territory, of economic life, and of a 'psychological make-up manifested in a community of culture'.[16] On the latter feature, Stalin proceeded to

---

[16] Joseph Stalin, 'Marxism and the National Question', in: *idem, Marxism and the National and Colonial Question*, London 1936, p. 8.

explain that nations differ with respect not only to their living conditions, but also to their 'spiritual complexion, which manifests itself in peculiarities of national culture'.[17] The less clearly elaborated 'psychological make-up', which other writers might describe as 'national character', takes, according to Stalin, many generations to emerge. As far as he was concerned, a nation did not exist until all four features were present: if one was absent, then the nation ceased to be. He demonstrated the contingency by pointing to the Baltic Germans and Latvians in Tsarist Russia. They did not constitute a nation in the nineteenth century despite their common territory and common economic life.[18] By dint of his involvement in the theoretical problems of the nation and nationalism, in 1917 Stalin was appointed the first Soviet 'Commissar of Nationalities', the post from which he began his rapid rise to absolute power.

In an effort to determine what a nation is, Hugh Seton-Watson, one of the most expert scholars of modern nationalism, has written that the members of a nation must feel they are bound together by a sense of solidarity, a common culture and a national consciousness. For him, a nation exists if 'a significant number of people in a community consider themselves to form a nation, or behave as if they formed one'.[19] He does not stipulate how large the community must be. Indeed he argues as a matter of principle that it is impossible to arrive at an exact scientific definition of a nation.

3 Cultural Nations and Political Nations

The distinction between cultural nation (*Kulturnation*) and political nation (*Staatsnation*) is one of the most famous contributions to enquiries into the nation, and one which is still most illuminating. The two German terms, for which neither English nor French knows exact equivalents, gained acceptance in the scholarly field thanks to the historian Friedrich Meinecke.[20] His basic premise was that the modern nation is principally founded upon equality or commonality, characteristics we noted above (see p. 7). The political nation centres on the idea of individual and collective self-determination. It derives from the individual's free will and subjective commitment to the nation. In the graphic, though rather dramatic, formulation offered by Ernest Renan, the French ecclesiastical historian, in 1882: 'The nation is a daily plebiscite'. In a lecture entitled '*Qu'est-ce qu'une nation*?' ('What is a nation?'), he examined the criteria usually employed to define nations and concluded that they were all inadequate; ultimately, the existence or otherwise of a nation depended on the will of the individuals: the population of a given, historically evolved territory perceives itself to be a nation, and citizenship is equated with

---

[17] *Ibid.*, p. 7.

[18] *Ibid.*, pp. 8–9.

[19] Hugh Seton-Watson, *Nations and States. An Enquiry into the Origins of Nations and the Politics of Nationalism*, London 1977, p. 5.

[20] Meinecke, *Cosmopolitanism and the National State*.

nationality. Seton-Watson's definition of the nation continues this tradition of thought.

By contrast, the spirit of community that obtains in a cultural nation is founded upon seemingly objective criteria such as common heritage and language, a distinct area of settlement, religion, customs and history, and does not need to be mediated by a national state or other political form. Consciousness of unity, the sense of belonging together, may develop independent of the state. The pre-political cultural nation can overarch existing particularistic state forms, such as in early nineteenth-century Germany and Italy. As the case of Poland between 1772 and 1918 shows, it can even outlast the long-term territorial division of a people into three multinational dynastic states. It leaves individuals little scope to choose to which nation they belong. It was hence quite logical that movements for national unity, which began to emerge in the nineteenth century, regarded the nation 'as an entity *preceding* the state and resting upon common historical or cultural values or social ties'.[21] The first steps towards transition to a political nation are taken when a cultural nation is politicized, and statist ideas take root within it.

The concept of political nation has its concrete historical referents in France, England and the United States, the latter being the classic land of multicultural immigration. In these three states, a process of domestic political transformation generated the nation as a community of politically aware citizens equal before the law irrespective of their social and economic status, ethnic origin and religious beliefs. In retrospect, the creation of modern France is looked upon as an act of will. The nation as a community of responsible citizens expressing a common political will through the state is constituted, in theory at least, by individual commitment to the ideas of 1789 and to the *grande patrie*. Nation and state are synonymous; the unifying whole is formed by a uniform language, a uniform judicial and administrative system, a central government and shared political ideals. The sovereignty of the people is the foundation of state power.

The cultural nation principle, which emphasizes common heritage and language, is characteristic of the emergence of nations in Central Europe, Italy and – with certain qualifications – East-Central Europe. Here the individual generally had little say as to which nation he or she belonged to. Membership of a nation was a fate decided by Nature and History. Thus the Western voluntarist, liberal-democratic concept of nation is contrasted by a deterministic one that is frequently deemed undemocratic and irrational.

Another pair of concepts, closely related to those of political nation and cultural nation, are now common usage in the literature on nationalism, largely as a result of the influential work done by the Prague-born American Hans Kohn. They are the west European and the east-central European concepts of nation; or subjective and objective concepts of

---

[21] Theodor Schieder, 'Typologie und Erscheinungsformen des Nationalstaats in Europa', in: *Historische Zeitschrift* 202 (1966), p. 63.

nation.[22] They are based on the same differential criteria that Meinecke adopted, and, essentially, refer to the same things.

Theories can easily maintain the conceptual distinctions between putative objective and subjective criteria to define the nation; in reality, of course, the boundaries between them are frequently crossed. For instance, to some people the Alsatians are German, because their culture and history, and in many respects their language too, assign them to the German cultural nation; to others they are French because of their desire to be citizens of the French state with which they have felt close ties since the Revolution of 1789 and the Napoleonic era, if not before. The political Swiss nation embraces three cultural nations – indeed four if we include the Romansch-speaking Rhaetians in Grisons. Even the French nation, the political nation *par excellence*, can be fully understood only with reference to a common language, culture and history. France does not only have the will of the nation – the 'General Will' – to thank for its political existence; 'France' is also the outcome of dynastic ambition, fortuitous political circumstances and diplomatic acumen. Closer inspection hence reveals that underlying the concept of the political nation there is always a lengthy process of convergence taking place within a larger state framework and, on occasion, receiving tremendous impetus from a state that pursues certain types of policies (the introduction of linguistic or judicial uniformity, for instance). All this is often ignored. Voluntary commitment to the nation *à la* Ernest Renan is meaningless in the absence of certain fundamental commonalities; the plebiscitary element is only one factor, although an important one, among many. In other words, the concept of nation represents an interlocking of objective actualities and the circumstance of subjective political will, an ever-changing combination whose shape is truly unique to each historical case.

In the first instance, peoples who had yet to gain their own common state, such as the Italians and Germans in the early nineteenth, and the Poles as late as the early twentieth century, invoked above all the common cultural and linguistic ground they shared. In doing so, they sought publicly to legitimate their claims for the identity between the cultural and the political nation within a nation-state. But even in these cases, the determined political will to erect a communal state was the ultimately decisive factor. This means that Renan's dictum about the daily plebiscite constituting the nation in a never-ending repeated process of integration applies just as well to Germans, Italians and Poles. At root, the freedom to choose and decide is a crucial condition for the existence of almost any type of social organization. Beyond this, theoretical justifications offered for the nation may vary as the interests of any given nation shift according to circumstances. For example, before 1918 Germans emphasized subjective, political factors in the case of East Prussian Masurians, who spoke a Polish dialect, and pointed to objective, cultural considerations where Alsatians were concerned. In each case the need was felt to prove that a minority was German or wanted to be citizens of the German nation-state.

---

[22] Kohn, *Idea of Nationalism*, pp. 455–576.

The nationalist thought that predominated in the Hungarian part of Austria-Hungary is also typical of this kind of opportunist argumentation. In the nineteenth century, the Magyars, pressing for the unification of the lands ruled by the crown of St Stephen, argued in terms of history and state structures, not of culture and language; they denied the non-Magyar minorities in the Kingdom of Hungary the right to decide their own destiny. The numerically larger Magyar linguistic nation presented itself as the dominant state nation and attempted forcibly to assimilate the various minorities, justifying their action on grounds of the democratic principle of majority will. All this suggests that the subjective concept of nation cannot simply be reserved for Western Europe, and its objective counterpart for East-Central and South-East Europe. The definitions are only workable if considerably qualified. What is clear, however, is that in nineteenth-century and, in particular, inter-war European national conflicts, 'nation' was in almost every case a function of ethnic, i.e., largely linguistic and cultural considerations.

What we find, then, is that it is extremely difficult to arrive at a generally valid definition of nation. But this conclusion does not absolve us from the need to specify the substance of a concept that will be frequently employed in the following. Proceeding from the various criteria noted above, a nation will be understood here as a social group (and by this we mean a people or a section of a people) which, because of a variety of historically evolved relations of a linguistic, cultural, religious or political nature, has become conscious of its coherence, political unity and particular interests. It demands the right to political self-determination, or has already achieved such through a nation-state. A *nation* is constituted by the social group's (the *people's*) consciousness of being a nation, or of wanting to be one, and by their demand for political self-determination. The nation is, furthermore, assigned a superior and more universal significance than other bodies of joint social action such as class, religious community or the family.

The fact that the urge for independent statehood is a core element in the above definition of nation suggests that while nation and state are not necessarily mutually dependent, they are at least closely connected. Linguistically, this becomes quite clear in French and English, where the word 'nation' can mean both 'nation' in its purest sense, and 'country' or 'state' (whereas German has retained the quite separate *Nation* and *Staat*). Contemporary international law has adopted the semantic links: the League of Nations (Société des Nations), created in 1920, and its successor the United Nations, formed in 1945, are organizations, not of peoples and nations, but of states.

A distinction should be made between 'nation' and the frequently encountered notion of 'nationality', which generally has a dual meaning. Following the definition of nation offered here, a nationality is a social group which regards itself as an ethnic minority within a given state and desires no more than respect as a separate community. It does not seek to wield political power in its own state, but it does strive for cultural and political autonomy within a broader state framework. Most of the individual nationalities in the Habsburg monarchy, for example, did not begin to yearn for separate states until the late nineteenth century. In addition, nationality is used, particularly in West European law, to mean citizenship: to which state one belongs.

4 National Consciousness and Nation-Building

National consciousness, the sense of belonging to a political and social community which constitutes – or wishes to constitute – a nation organized as a state, is the fundamental basis of the cultural or political nation. In principle, national consciousness is independent of the existence of a national state; without national consciousness, however, a national movement would be doomed to failure. National consciousness is mediated by education in the widest sense of the word, and can undergo transformation as much as the values, objects and symbols to which it refers. In the development of national consciousness, social groups emphasize the various commonalities we have mentioned – language, culture, religion, political ideals, history – and tone down other local or universal political or religious ties that might sap their unity. The loyalties may also be to an existing state, or one that used to exist and whose erstwhile site is now seen as the people's historic homeland. In addition, social groups also tend to define their national identity and national consciousness in negative terms, i.e., through distinction from or comparison with neighbours. Encounters with the 'alien' – other forms of language, religion, customs, political systems – make people aware of the close ties, shared values and common ground that render communication with their own kind so much easier than with outsiders.

National consciousness can be directed, at least temporarily, against a presumed enemy, another nation, or the existing multinational state in which the social group or nation lives. This is particularly true of peoples still struggling for their own nation-state such as the Germans and Italians in the nineteenth century. Napoleonic rule, perceived by many as heteronomy and oppression, sparked off German political national consciousness in the early nineteenth century. The national movement in Germany matured between 1806 and 1813, though it was initially the child of an intellectual élite. After 1815, the irrefutably anti-French leanings of German national consciousness waned, particularly since after the July Revolution of 1830 early German liberalism extolled France as the home of the free and constitutional political order. Only when France re-embarked upon an expansionist policy eastwards, encroaching upon the Rhine border and thereby calling into question the Germans' title to a part of their 'historic' homeland, did German national consciousness rediscover a Francophobic tenor. It was to predominate for almost a hundred years. National passions aroused by the Rhine crisis in 1840 produced songs such as Max Schneckenburg's 'The Watch on the Rhine', Nikolaus Becker's 'They Shall Not Take the Free German Rhine', and August Heinrich Hoffmann von Fallersleben's 'Song of Germany' (later to become the national anthem). It was not long before the Rhine songs were being sung all over Germany. Around 1840 a campaign to finish the gothic cathedral at Cologne emerged, orchestrated by numerous pressure groups and accompanied by a wealth of popular publications. The incomplete church had become a major symbol of an incomplete German national unity. Cologne cathedral thus became Germany's national monument, its construction a cause for all Germans. To a great extent it was a symbol of liberation from and resistance to French domination, for France's policy *vis-à-vis* the Rhine in 1840 had rekindled memories of 1813.[23] The Prussian King Frederick William IV was at the centre of the grand ceremony held on 4 September 1842 to celebrate the campaign for the completion of the cathedral.

In the 1840s, the anti-French strain of German national consciousness was paralleled by anti-Danish sentiments fired until 1864 by the Danish–German conflict over Schleswig and Holstein. Here two nationalisms clashed, with 'Schleswig-Holstein Embraced by the Sea' becoming the appropriate German battle song. By the late nineteenth century German national consciousness was presented with the further problem of the imperial power of Britain. Britain joined the ranks of those countries obstructing Germany's now worldwide national interests – or so Imperial Germany liked to believe, especially the power élites who spread fears of political and military 'encirclement'.

Nineteenth-century Italian national consciousness was inspired by the glory of Ancient Rome and by the enmity of the Habsburg monarchy, which the political and military leadership of Piedmont, with French support, managed gradually to repel from the Italian peninsula after 1859. For the peoples of the southern Balkans, the struggle against Ottoman Turkey up until the First World War remained an important ingredient of their national consciousness; for the Irish, it was conflict with England; while for the Poles, the catalyst of national fervour was resistance against the dividing powers of Russia, Prussia/Germany and Austria-Hungary. Likewise, in many of the African and Asian states that emerged after 1945, the fight against European colonialism and imperialism was the origin of a national consciousness which in most cases had yet to be created. Not infrequently, 'wars of liberation' waged against white colonial masters and their stooges engendered for the first time among the colonized peoples the sense that they all shared a common political fate, irrespective of their manifest differences.

In the case of some European peoples, prototypes of national consciousness and nationalist discourse can be identified as early as the fourteenth century and even before. The works of Petrarch, Dante or Shakespeare are also commonly cited as convincing evidence of early national consciousness, as is the final chapter of Machiavelli's *The Prince* of 1513, which exhorts the Italians to liberate themselves from the barbarians and become again a united country. In general the only conclusion that can sensibly be drawn is that it is practically impossible to place an exact date on when a social group or people first conceives of itself as a nation. Apart

---

[23] Thomas Nipperdey, 'Der Kölner Dom als Nationaldenkmal', in: Otto Dann (ed.), *Religion – Kunst – Vaterland. Der Kölner Dom im 19. Jahrhundert*, Cologne 1983, pp. 109–110.

from a few exceptions, the nation is a goal rather than an actuality. Put simply, nations are not creatures of 'God's hand', as post-Herder prophets of nationalism often claimed; instead they are synthetic – they have to be created in a complicated educational process. They are 'imagined communities' (Benedict Anderson). The French philosopher Roland Barthes even goes so far as to deny nations historical reality, preferring to assign them to the realm of political myth.[24]

The rather inscrutable process of nation-building, engineered by intellectual minorities but directed at the social group as a whole, is generally an extremely drawn-out process of social and political integration. It can never be deemed complete, even after a nation has gained its own independent state. A political consciousness capable of successfully containing internal conflict does not evolve in a unilinear fashion; its development is constantly being dogged by delays and setbacks. The aim of nation-building is to integrate and harmonize socially, regionally or even politically and institutionally divided sections of a people. The motives underlying nation-building are various, and shaped by the historical and political environment. In recent times – and not surprisingly – nationalism as an ideology and political movement has been a significant part of the process. Its success always depends primarily on the establishment of a consciousness that can bind the special character of a value or political cause to a particular 'national' group, and define its 'uniqueness' as the substance of a national ideology. Nation-building and nationalism, which Elie Kedourie has succinctly described as 'a method of teaching the right determination of the will',[25] are hence inextricably linked. Since they obviously mean and refer to different things, it would seem sensible to make a sharper distinction than has hitherto been the case in the relevant literature, between nation-building as a basic process, and nationalism as an ideology and political movement.

National consciousness can also be promoted, and nations created, by a determined state whose general modes are centralization, uniformity and efficiency. Nation-building then proceeds within a framework identical with the state's frontiers. This was, for example, the case in early France, England, Portugal and Sweden, where state-building went hand in hand with, though probably preceded, nation-building. On closer inspection, the populations living within the borders of the states where the kings of France, England or Sweden were the respective sovereigns, became nations. The French nation, for instance, embraces population groups of varying origins, cultures, and even languages. The nation – the political nation – was created 'from above', as it were, more or less according to the principle of *cuius regio eius natio*. National consciousness was oriented around real frontiers. By contrast with France, which was largely successful on this count, sprawling imperial bodies interlocked by dynastic interests, such as the Habsburg monarchy and, to a certain extent, Tsarist

---

[24] Roland Barthes, *Mythologies*, Paris 1957, pp. 155–61.
[25] Elie Kedourie, *Nationalism*, London 1961, p. 81.

Russia, managed to engender a stunted imperial national consciousness among no more than a few narrow strata of society.

Nineteenth and early twentieth-century Europe saw how in many other instances the process of nation-building set in before nation-states came about. It often transcended existing frontiers, rendering them obsolete, and led ultimately to the formation of new states with new frontiers. Shared language and culture underlay this process, the goal of which was the cohesion of the cultural nation in a *single* state: in other words, political, linguistic and cultural congruence. Consequently it can be said that the emergence of a national movement indicates that a population or social group has reached a new stage on the road to nationhood: the transition to political action. The nation, or the sections of a population that consider themselves to be a nation, attempt to create their own state. Examples of national forces that were blessed with propitious political circumstances are the Greek, Italian, German, Irish and Polish movements. But even in these cases it is unclear how far nation-building had proceeded when the nation-state was actually established. After the Italians had succeeded in forming a nation-state in 1861, Massimo d'Azeglio, the writer and former prime minister of Piedmont, mindful in particular of the conflict between northern and southern Italy, is supposed to have remarked: 'We have made Italy: now we have to make Italians'.[26] D'Azeglio was thus acutely aware that political unification in the national state did not automatically guarantee the existence of the nation. By contrast, a condition of any organized national movement aspiring to create a nation-state is the existence of at least the first stages of nation-building and a national consciousness.

---

[26] Quoted in Seton-Watson, *Nations and States*, p. 107. See also Klaus Zernack, 'Germans and Poles: Two Cases of Nation-Building', in: Hagen Schulze (ed.), *Nation-Building in Central Europe*, Leamington Spa 1987, pp. 149–66.

2

Emancipation and Oppression: Towards a Typology of Nationalism

1 The Spectrum of Historical Experience

During its first flourishing in early nineteenth-century Europe, modern nationalism was seen as a force that would enable the peoples of the continent to cast off the fetters of their political and social bondage. As the ideology which inscribed self-determination and equality upon the flags of peoples, nationalism supplied the demand for independent statehood with its legitimation. It awakened enthusiasm, hopes and expectations.

One of the leading personalities in the Greek independence movement – one of the first of its type – Prince Alexander Ypsilantis, who was in the military service of the Russian Tsar, penned a stirring appeal to his compatriots in February 1821 at the beginning of the Greek revolt against Ottoman rule. He wrote:

> 'Just raise your eyes, comrades! Behold your pitiful condition, your desecrated temples, your daughters delivered up to the lust of barbarians, your plundered houses, your devastated fields, you yourselves living as wretched slaves! Has the time not come to throw off this unbearable yoke and free the fatherland? Cast aside all that is alien, wave the flag, make the sign of the cross and you will surely triumph and save the fatherland and our religion from the blasphemy of the pagans. Which of you, noble Greeks, will not with a glad heart seek to free the fatherland from its chains?' The appeal continued: 'Above all, however, your sense of community must prevail. The rich among you must contribute a part of their wealth, the priests must encourage the people by teaching and example, and those civilian and military personnel serving at foreign courts must resign their duties under whatever regime they find themselves. They must all strive together towards the great goal, and thereby pay off their old debt to the fatherland. As is fitting for men of noble race, they must all arm themselves without delay and I promise them victory in short order and with it the advent of all happiness. Stand up as a bold people against those decadent slaves, those hirelings, and show yourselves to be true descendants of the heroes of classical times.'[1]

---

[1] Quoted in R. Ruland (ed.), *Restauration und Fortschritt*, Munich 1963, pp. 46–47.

Like the other peoples of the Balkans, the Greeks had at that stage been under Turkish rule for centuries. As Christians, they suffered discrimination in the Sultan's empire and yet they occupied key positions in the economy and even in the administration. Their situation was insecure, but not unbearable. There were colonies of Greek merchants and traders in all the larger cities of the eastern Mediterranean under Ottoman rule. Although the Greeks drew significant economic advantage from their unhindered freedom of movement in the Ottoman Empire, aspirations towards greater political freedom stirred among them, as they did among their northern neighbours as Ottoman central government progressively declined. From the late eighteenth century onwards, under the influence of the French Revolution and its ideas, there had been outbreaks of guerilla warfare and revolt against the Turks, the first result of which had been the acquisition of a limited political autonomy by Serbia in 1815.

The Serbian success encouraged the Greeks to press forward their struggle for a change in the political status quo in the regions which they considered to be Greek territory. Ypsilantis' appeal is a typical example of these aspirations and the colourful rhetoric that accompanied them. The arguments presented in his appeal were repeated with only minor variations in the programmes of the other national movements in nineteenth-century Europe. Even later they appear with thoroughly tiresome monotony, right up to the anti-colonial liberation movements in Asia and Africa since the First World War. What were these arguments?

Ypsilantis' clarion call to struggle against alien Ottoman rule appealed to the solidarity of the people, the deeds of the mythical heroes of its history and the willingness of individuals to sacrifice themselves. Ypsilantis demanded unconditional service to the fatherland and urged a consciousness of 'Greekness', whatever he might have understood by that. He promised victory over the Turks and 'with it the advent of all happiness'. In so doing, he was attempting quite openly to arouse hopes of a better life in an independent Greek state. This state, however, as an economic unit (and this was already easy to see at the time) would offer the Greeks substantially less potential for development than the Ottoman Empire, which stretched over three continents. Economics did not, however, enter into it at the time. The superordinate goal of Greek nationalism, a Greek nation-state, took precedence over all other considerations. In the 1820s, the Greeks seemed to have drawn palpably nearer their goal as their struggle for liberation had found sympathy and support in Europe. Above all, the liberal political public of Western and Central Europe saw in nationalism an effective means of transforming congealed political and social conditions in the oppressive years of Restoration after the Congress of Vienna.

Some 130 years after the inception of the movement for Greek independence from Turkish rule, nationalism was still being regarded as a revolutionary force by the peoples of Africa and Asia. In Western Europe, meanwhile, it had undergone a startling re-evaluation since the days of Prince Ypsilantis. There it was no longer seen as the overture and accompaniment to a 'springtime of the peoples' nor as a force that could lead

Europe towards a better future and create a more peaceful order among nations. In the middle of the twentieth century, nationalism had become a destructive force with horrific associations. For the people of Europe, nationalism now signified as Johan Huizinga put it, primarily 'the powerful drive to dominate', the 'urge to have one's own nation, one's own state assert itself above, over, and at the cost of others'.[2] Konrad Adenauer, the first chancellor of the Federal Republic of Germany, called nationalism 'the cancerous sore of Europe'.[3] After the Second World War, the vast majority of Europeans equated nationalism with bellicose aggression, the unbridled urge for expansion, and racism. They regarded it as the expression of a blinkered mentality which had brought immeasurable calamity down upon Europe.

> 'Of all the evils I hate I think I hate nationalism most', wrote the British publisher and author Victor Gollancz in his autobiography of 1952. 'Nationalism – national egoism, thinking in terms of one's nation rather than in terms of humanity – nationalism is evil because it concentrates on comparative inessentials (where a man lives, what sort of language he speaks, the type of his culture, the character of his "blood") and ignores the essential, which is simply that he is a man ... It makes one set of people hate another set that they haven't the smallest real occasion for hating: it leads to jealousy, expansionism, oppression, strife and eventually war.'[4]

Gollancz lived at a time when nationalism had entirely shed its original emancipatory and liberal character and had turned out to be an extreme ideology with disastrous consequences for the co-existence of the European peoples. German and Italian nationalism, in particular, had advocated a programme of oppression, and even annihilation, of other peoples, and in the 1930s and 1940s had translated words into action. To Europeans, having experienced the perverted nationalism of Fascist Italy and National Socialist Germany, it represented a morally reprehensible phenomenon.

The negative evaluation of nationalism after 1945, so unmistakable in Gollancz's writings, still largely determines current Western European opinion on nationalism. Even its earlier manifestations are in retrospect judged in these moral tones. The change in attitude is particularly evident among Germans, for whom nationalism was thoroughly discredited after the last war. They had seen the nationalism of Wilhelmine Germany culminate in the First World War, and knew how the excesses of Third Reich ultra-nationalism, with its radical racial policies, had led to the destruction of the German national state, itself founded only in 1871. This complete reversal of attitude subsequently encouraged in the western part of Germany a tendency to underestimate the continuing significance of nationalism in other areas of the world. To consider nationalism and

---

[2] Johan Huizinga, *Men and Ideas. Essays on History, the Middle Ages, the Renaissance*, New York 1959, p. 97.
[3] Konrad Adenauer, *Erinnerungen 1945–1953*, vol. 1, 2nd ed., Stuttgart 1973, p. 425.
[4] Victor Gollancz, *My Dear Timothy. An Autobiographical Letter to his Grandson*, Harmondsworth 1952, pp. 294–95.

its history chiefly in terms of National Socialism and the self-emasculation of Europe through two world wars, however, prevents deeper understanding. As a political principle that is currently more crucial than ever in determining the foreign and domestic policies of many countries, and which has retained its power to mobilize the masses against internal and external opposition, nationalism is still far from irrelevant.

2 Risorgimento Nationalism

The words of Ypsilantis and Gollancz show that 'nationalism' can be associated with a whole range of conceptions, expectations and experiences. Both – one a Greek, the other a Briton – can talk of nationalism, but their attitudes to it could hardly diverge more. This underscores the definitional confusion surrounding the term. The great variety of roles nationalism has played in specific historical contexts can serve as a starting point for a typology classifying these diverse forms systematically into two main groups or basic types: Risorgimento nationalism and integral nationalism. Though it runs the risk of oversimplifying matters, this kind of historical, functional-based typology treats nationalism as a value-free, analytical category and tries to get away from moral judgements of 'good' and 'evil'. Notwithstanding the generalizations it entails, it is of considerable value as a heuristic device for describing and explaining the complex phenomenon of nationalism.

In order to gain an overall, keynote grasp of Risorgimento nationalism, of which Ypsilantis is a typical exponent, it can for the moment be defined as an emancipatory political force. It accompanies the liberation both of new social strata within an existing, formerly absolutist Western European state, and of a people that has grown conscious of itself in opposition to a transnational ruling power in East-Central Europe. Risorgimento nationalism, frequently referred to as 'liberal nationalism', 'genuine nationalism', or 'nationalism in its original phase', serves as a medium for the political fusion of large social groups, the formation of nations and their self-identification in the national state. The ultimate goal of Risorgimento nationalism, whose historical model is nineteenth-century Italian nationalism, is liberation from political and social oppression. It comprises unmistakable elements of a liberal ideology of opposition. It is a protest movement against an existing system of political domination, against a state which destroys the nation's traditions and prevents it flourishing. Its adherents stress the right of every nation, and with it the right of *each* and *every* member of a nation, to autonomous and equal development, for in their minds, individual freedom and national independence are closely connected. The national movement in early nineteenth-century Germany, for instance, therefore campaigned for civil freedoms too. On 27 January 1822, the Greek constitutional national assembly, which sat in Epidaurus, issued a declaration to the peoples of Europe. It read:

> The war which we are carrying on against the Turk is not that of a faction or the result of sedition. It is not aimed at the advantage of any single part

of the Greek people; it is a national war, a holy war, a war the object of which is to reconquer the rights of individual liberty, of property and honour, – rights which the civilized people of Europe, our neighbours, enjoy today; rights of which the cruel and unheard of tyranny of the Ottomans would deprive us – us alone – and the very memory of which they would stifle in our hearts.'[5]

Influential prophets of liberal Risorgimento nationalism, such as the German Johann Gottfried Herder and the Italian Giuseppe Mazzini, believed that peoples so evidently different in language and character also had unique duties to perform for humanity: each of them had a mission. Their philosophy could be traced directly to French nationalism in the late eighteenth and early nineteenth centuries, for French revolutionaries again and again justified their nationalism in terms of their mission to propagate the universal human ideals of liberty, equality and fraternity throughout Europe. At the time this was felt to lend French nationalism a higher meaning. Similarly, Mazzini, who for a while had lived in exile in France, believed that England's 'calling' was to industrialize and create overseas colonies, Russia's to civilize Asia, Germany's to philosophize, and Italy's to lead the world as the 'third Rome'.

In 1857, Mazzini produced a map of his 'ideal Europe'. It comprised but eleven nations. He denied some of Europe's less numerous peoples the right to their own national state, refusing to accept them as nations. The Irish, he argued for instance, essentially needed better government; they lacked the fundamental characteristics of the nation, such as language and national customs, as well as a unique historic mission, a specific duty in the noble service of humanity. Mazzini advised them to be content as an integral part of the United Kingdom.[6] His views naturally did not only enrage Irish nationalists, even if in retrospect they sound naive and lacking in historical substance. But in Mazzini's days, such thinking was not unimportant in lending legitimacy and ideological cogency to Risorgimento nationalism.

It was recognized that a people was incapable of fulfilling its rather divine mission, whose generally nebulous contours emerge through a process of national myth-building, unless it was free. In place of the war-torn world of the *ancien régime*, Mazzini offered an ideal of friendship that straddled frontiers, linking all free nations irrespective of their size and power. The old Europe of restored monarchies would be superseded by the young Europe of emancipated nations created as they were by God's intervention in language and geography. Once established, the order of nation-states would guarantee peace, for it would satisfy the will, not only of the peoples, but of God too.

In its theoretical form, this was a convincing vision of a more humane and peaceful world order founded upon the plurality of free nations; but in the real world of politics, those who attempted to implement it ran up

---

[5] Printed in: Hans Kohn (ed.), *Nationalism: Its Meaning and History*, 2nd ed., Princeton (NJ) 1965, pp. 116–17.
[6] Nicholas Mansergh, *The Irish Question 1840–1921*, 2nd ed., London 1965, pp. 76–80.

against unassailable obstacles. Not only was there resistance on the part of the multinational imperial powers, which rightly regarded the principle of the nation-state as a declaration of war on their very existence; conflicts between the various nationalisms were built into the scheme from the very start by the maxim of equality between all nations and their political aspirations. There were bound to be clashes between national ambitions in areas such as the Balkan peninsula and large parts of East-Central Europe, where peoples who regarded themselves as nations lived almost on top of one another, as well as in places where the dominant nation of a large state sought to inhibit the development of other nationalisms. The history of the multinational Habsburg Empire up to its dissolution in 1918 abounds in evidence of the rise of 'sub-nationalisms', most especially in the Hungarian half of the country. There, after 1875, a radical policy of Magyarization was pursued, partly as a reaction to powerful Viennese influence within the monarchy as a whole. In turn, Magyar nationalism, which took linguistic unity of the Hungarian lands as a platform, provoked a national reaction among Slovaks, Croats, Germans and Romanians. Magyar rejection of the Habsburg embrace collided with the rejection of Magyar nationalism by the nationalities living in Hungary.[7]

Evidence of a dominant nationalism aiming to assimilate others is provided by the Russification policies of the Tsarist government from the 1860s onwards in the Russian part of Poland, in the Baltic provinces of the Empire, in the Ukraine and later in Finland. In 1887, Russian was made compulsory as the language of instruction in all state schools in the Baltic provinces, a measure later extended to private schools as well. Another example is the Prussian policy of Germanization in the province of Posen in the 1830s and then again in the 1870s. The goal of such policies was linguistic unification of the existing state, and their architects did not rule out the ruthless use of pressure and force. Underlying them was, after all, the widely held conviction that nationality was primarily a function of language, and the character of a nation-state was manifested by a single national tongue.

In general, however, Risorgimento nationalism, particularly its earlier forms, upheld the principle of solidarity of the oppressed against the oppressors. It did not pit nation against nation, but united all nations against the tyrant – whether this be a single minor prince, a dynastic power or a multinational empire: the Holy Alliance of the peoples faced the Holy Alliance of the princes. Nineteenth-century national movements lent each other intellectual and in some cases also material support, but only insofar as their nationalisms did not clash. Like the anti-colonial liberation movements of the twentieth, the nationalists of the first half of the nineteenth century constituted an International. Nationally-minded Europeans were excited by the Greeks' struggle to throw off Ottoman rule in the 1820s. The political enthusiasm surrounding 'the rebirth of Greece', as the German professor of philosophy Wilhelm Traugott Krug phrased it in 1821, propelled the formation of volunteers brigades and pro-Greek

---

[7] Robert A. Kann, *A History of the Habsburg Empire 1526–1918*, Berkeley (Calif.) 1974, pp. 452–67, 538–44.

pressure groups, and inspired fervent literary and artistic activity. Lord Byron became famous the length and breadth of the continent, even though he died in 1824 shortly after arriving in Greece with magnificent ceremony. The unfulfilled yearnings of other nations, particularly in Central Europe, were grafted onto the political and literary Philhellenism now abroad, and it is easy to spot the traces of Christianity and new humanism it embraced.

After 1830–31, it was the turn of the Poles to be celebrated as the vanguard of political and national liberalism. Following the failure of another revolt against the suppressive Tsarist regime many had emigrated to Western Europe. Poles saw themselves as the victims of Tsarist auto-cracy in Russia and as the martyrs in the cause of European freedom. Poland was the 'Christ among the peoples'; but the 'crucified nation', as the poet Adam Mickiewicz put it, would rise again; its liberation would herald the liberation of the whole of humanity from war and oppression. The notion was not novel; the Polish legions formed by Henryk Dabrowski in 1797 had fought under the motto 'For freedom ours and yours'. Enthusiasm and friendship for Poland became a major characteristic of Germans sympathetic to the causes of liberalism, nation-alism and democracy, and this contrasted starkly with the anti-Polish stance which the Prussian and Austrian governments had adopted after the Polish uprising in the Congress Kingdom in 1830–31. Between 1830 and 1848, the cause of German freedom and unity and Polish national independence seemed to be almost the same thing.

Nationalists formed international organizations in the 1830s and 1840s: in Switzerland in 1834 Mazzini formed a secret society called *La Giovine Europa* (Young Europe), which, with its Italian, Polish and German sec-tions, supported the European movements for national liberation and was to form the heart of the federation of free nations he dreamed of.[8] The founding of The Democratic Friends of All Nations in 1844 in London was followed a year later by The Fraternal Democrats, which had Polish, Irish and German members, and by The People's International League in 1847. These mostly short-lived associations were meant to cement political and practical solidarity between nationalists of liberal-democratic persuasion. However, international Risorgimento nationalism had no blue-print to hand for avoiding the growing number of situations in which the com-peting aims of different nationalisms were hopelessly at loggerheads.

It is possible to distinguish types of liberal, reformist Risorgimento nationalism, which had its heyday in Europe between the Congress of Vienna in 1814–15 and the Paris Peace Conference in 1919, according to whether its particular emancipatory component primarily addresses the realm of human co-existence, determined by the acquisition and exercise of power ('political nationalism'), or whether it is chiefly concerned with economic policy ('economic nationalism'). By analogy, we might talk of 'cultural nationalism' in cases where the emancipatory drive derives from concerns about culture, language, art, literature and education. We should

---

[8] Harry Hearder, *Italy in the Age of the Risorgimento 1790–1870*, London 1990, pp. 189–90.

further note that language and religion can become such burning issues that we can justifiably speak of 'linguistic' and 'religious' nationalism. All these various possible forms of Risorgimento nationalism are interdependent. In most of the historical examples known to us, political nationalism has eventually dominated, reinforced by economic or cultural nationalism, and hence assigned these less dominant national aspirations an auxilliary function in the consolidation of national consciousness. In many instances, however, cultural or economic preceded political nationalism. The reverse was less frequently the case. Ireland is an example, where cultural and economic nationalism did not become important until the end of the nineteenth century, giving a completely new dimension and direction to the political nationalism that had already been active for a long time.

Depending upon its political goal, Risorgimento nationalism can be designated unifying nationalism where it seeks to create the national state by fusing together politically divided parts, or secessionist nationalism if its aim is to separate a nation from a multinational dynastic empire. Examples of the former type in nineteenth and early twentieth-century Europe are the Italian and German national movements, and of the latter the Greek, Czech, Finnish and Irish. The Polish movement, which hoped to sever Polish areas from Russia, Austria-Hungary and Prussia/Germany and unite them in one restored Polish state, illustrates probably most clearly a nationalism that had both secessionist and unifying ambitions.

3 Reform Nationalism

Some aspects of Risorgimento nationalism are related to another type, reform nationalism, which arose mainly in Asia in the second half of the nineteenth century. Both aspired to the rebirth of some type of state. But by contrast with Risorgimento nationalism, reform nationalism emerged in an existing state that proved inferior in certain economic, technical and military respects when confronted by Western powers.

Although many of these frequently very old Asian states had not been subject to formal Western political control, contact with the Occident called forth a nationalism that anticipated many of the features of twentieth-century anti-colonial nationalism. Reform nationalism grew out of a position of defence, asserting itself against outside economic control, foreign cultural influence and political tutelage. At the same time, it studied and adopted Western models in order to modernize political and economic life within the existing social order and to rejuvenate its sclerotic administrative structures. The exponents of reform nationalism endeavoured to retain traditional social values and norms and to protect the threatened independence of the state by reforming society, the economy, the armed forces and governmental structures. This difficult operation, whose aim was the creation of a modern nation-state, was carried out using a tool imported from the West – national ideology. History's best-known examples of reform nationalism are Japan and Turkey, and, with some qualification, China, Egypt and Iran after 1921.

The bearers of reform nationalism in these countries mainly belonged to the traditional ruling strata: the upper echelons of the bureaucracy, the nobility, and the military. At first, pressure for reform was directed almost exclusively towards military affairs and the administrative structure of the existing state. It grew from the understandable desire to improve the country's capability of fending off the Western military threat. But the reform of just single, isolated sectors of society soon proved inadequate. The realization that this was so quickly caused modernization programmes to become ever more wide-ranging. In response to conservative resistance at home, which was bound to ensue, reformists invoked the national interest and the need to defend national identity, the national heritage and independence from the threat of the outside world. The control by the reformists of key governmental positions was absolutely crucial for the ultimate success of what in the end amounted to a revolution from above. This happened in the Meiji Era between 1868 and 1912 in Japan, the best and most successful example of an ossified state and society that managed to modernize along Western lines and under a nationalist ethos. The less impressive enterprise of Turkish reform nationalism, likewise launched in the late nineteenth century, failed to bear fruit until after the Ottoman Empire collapsed in the First World War and the Sultan was removed in 1923.

Reform nationalism in Japan was inflamed by a demonstration of power by the American fleet in Tokyo Bay in 1853 in conjunction with a trade treaty, signed reluctantly by the Japanese at Kanagawa in 1854 and giving American ships the right to use Japanese ports. Similar 'unequal treaties' with European powers followed. It was this traumatic experience of involuntary contact with the outside world that lay behind the extensive programme of reforms propagated by bureaucratic élites in Japan from the late 1860s onwards. Within a few decades they managed to transform a Japan that by Western standards was an underdeveloped and militarily weak feudal state, into an industrial and regional military power which by 1905 was strong enough to defeat the great European might of Russia.

The fundamental reforms of the army, administration, law and the economy that occurred during the Meiji Era proceeded under the motto 'Restoration of the Imperial Rule': in other words, the reformists hoped to latch on to a venerable institution in Japan's political system that the shoguns had been pushing into the background since the twelfth century. Consequently, when the last shogun was deposed in 1867 the Emperor became the focal point of the campaign for national renewal whose rhetoric urged that the path to true patriotism was willingness to make every sacrifice for him, the symbol of the nation's identity and independence. But the Emperor could only rise to popular glory and defend the nation's sovereignty if his country opened its gates to the modern world and adopted many of its ways. The reformists thus threw a veil over the radical changes they introduced into Japan's life and political system by emphasizing national traditions and warning of the threat to the country's independence. In so doing, they were able to marginalize opposition. Originally a reaction to the military and political challenge posed by the West, nationalism became a vehicle of integration as modernization and industrialization engendered social destabilization and mobilization. As an ideology it conjoined endeavours to maintain Japanese identity and independence with the recognition that Japan's backward society had to be reshaped in order to match the technical standards of Western civilization. The stress on continuity was meant to offset the inevitable discontinuities due to occur in the process.

Ottoman Turkey was also exposed to massive intervention by foreign powers after the mid-nineteenth century. The political cohesion of the multinational empire, stretching from the Balkans, to Asia Minor, to Palestine and North Africa, had been progressively weakened by the separatist nationalism of the Christian Balkan peoples, and then later by the Arabs. Revolution in 1908–09 by the Young Turks, who had built support mainly in the armed forces and the educated strata, many of whom had been educated in the West, formally signalled the end of the Sultan's autocratic rule. But it was only with Kemalism's project of political and cultural reform that the foundation stone for a European-type Turkish national state was laid, and this itself was only possible after the break-up of the Ottoman Empire. The intellectual and political leader of reformism, which embraced a wider social base after the First World War, was the Macedonian-born professional army officer Mustafa Kemal, known as Kemal Atatürk after 1934. In Anatolia in May 1919 he had begun to organize resistance to Allied and Greek occupation of parts of the country. A kind of xenophobia and fears of external threats were as important a spur in Turkish reform nationalism as they had been in late nineteenth-century Japan. Kemalism was the hallmark of a programme of national regeneration for the Republic proclaimed in October 1923. It was an ideology that thrust Turkey forward under the flag of secularization and 'Europeanization'.

Despite their patent similarities, we should not overlook the obvious differences between Japanese and Turkish reform nationalism. While traditional concepts and symbols were central to the former, the Turks explicitly inveighed against key values from the past. For instance, they brushed aside fierce criticism from conservatives and denied the unity of state and religion that is anchored in Islam; they abolished the caliphate in 1924; they transferred the capital from Istanbul to Ankara; and they opposed the wearing of the fez and the veil. They would free the Turkish language from the influence of Arabic and bring it nearer to the vernacular so that broad sections of the awakening nation would be able to read and understand literature. In 1929 Arabic and Farsi were struck from the curricula of secondary education and replaced by Latin and Greek. All these steps suggest that post-war Turkey was concerned with more than a mere reform of existing state and society; it was *de facto* a question of reconstructing a state based on the concept of the nation and deriving from the heritage of the multinational Ottoman Empire. The reconstruction or state-building from scratch required revolutionary intervention and a partial break with the values and norms of the pre-national past: for the old structures of society and domination were obstructing the *risorgimento* of the Turkish nation.

4 Integral Nationalism

Integral nationalism, the counter-type to Risorgimento nationalism, is encountered under various names. Radical; extreme; militant; aggressive-expansionist; derivative; right-wing; reactionary; excessive: these are just a few of the more common adjectives attached to the term. They clearly show that a generally accepted nomenclature for the typology of nationalism does not exist. The term 'integral nationalism' will be preferred here, despite some reservations. It was coined by the French writer Charles Maurras, one of the most influential intellectual founding-fathers of this type of nationalism. In the years before the First World War, Maurras propagated an all-embracing nationalism as a substitute religion culminating in a mystical cult of the earth and the dead that made absolute demands of the individual.[9] Integral nationalism casts off all ethical ballast, obligating and totally subordinating the individual to one value alone, the nation. 'La France d'abord', 'My country, right or wrong', 'You are nothing, your people everything', are the kinds of moral commands to which integral nationalism binds the faithful and with which it legitimizes the potential use of physical violence against the heretic and minorities.

In complete contrast to Risorgimento nationalism, which proceeds from the notion that all nationalisms and the claims of all national movements are equal, integral nationalism defines the one nation as the Absolute. It is not justified by its followers in terms of service for a higher cause; the cult of the nation becomes an end in itself. In place of the humanist ideas of a Herder or a Mazzini, the skimpy philosophical foundation of integral nationalism is provided by Darwin's theory of natural selection and the doctrine of the survival of the fittest. As far as the prophets of integral nationalism are concerned, what goes for animals and individuals must also go for races and nations. The nation that proves itself as the strongest and fittest in a hostile and competing world shall gain the upper hand and ultimately survive. While for Herder and Mazzini the awakening of nations meant the unfurling of a new, peaceful world order, for integral nationalism it merely exacerbates the battle of all against all. Hence Risorgimento nationalism is totally different. This is also true with respect to individuals: Mussolini and Hitler, for example, represent a type of nationalist quite distinct from Ypsilantis or Mazzini.

Exponents of integral nationalism are prepared unscrupulously to assert the interests of their own nation at the expense of others. The interests themselves are defined and interpreted by the foremost political figure, the 'leader'. 'Il duce ha sempre ragione' – the leader is always right – as was said in Italy in the 1920s and 1930s. Absolute devotion to the nation became the guiding principle of Fascist education. The existence of other nations was questioned, or even denied. In integral nationalism, slogans about national supremacy, and the superiority of one's own nation, replaced the maxims of national self-determination and equality that in the

---

[9] W. C. Buthman, *The Rise of Integral Nationalism in France with Special Reference to the Ideas and Activities of Charles Maurras*, 2nd ed., New York 1970. Eugen Weber, *The Nationalist Revival in France, 1905–1914*, Berkeley (Calif.) 1968.

decades after the French Revolution had given such enormous dynamism to Risorgimento nationalism. It is as if at a certain historical juncture a boiling point is reached, and nationalism enters into a new chemical state; the pattern of values and norms that had obtained hitherto shifts to a new paradigm. What is now 'ethical' and morally justified is whatever serves the nation and its power; for that higher purpose injustice, even crime, is acceptable. Here lie the roots of relentless persecution and violation of the law, of expansionist foreign policy and the unbridled ambitions of a 'master race' seeking *Lebensraum*, of the compulsory expulsion of people from their homelands and of genocide that have been perpetrated in the twentieth century in the name of the nation.

The early advocates of Risorgimento nationalism had, with prophet-like clarity, already occasionally realized that nationalist thought might contain the seeds of transgression of moral boundaries. The Age of Revolution in France had indeed provided a foretaste of what was to come. The radical Jacobin hybrid of nationalism in the Revolution had already acquired totalitarian traits: the nation was *'une et indivisible'* – one and indivisible, egalitarian and homogeneous. Anyone who resisted its demands would be dispatched with force if necessary. In the putative interests of the nation, the Jacobins clamped down on dissent, pluralism, federalism and autonomous institutions like the church. The zenith of this development in France was the erection of altars dedicated to the fatherland. Hitherto, the pious citizen had thanked his god for life and well-being; now he learned that he owed everything to the nation. 'There is something terrible in the sacred love of the fatherland', conceded Louis Antoine Saint-Just, a supporter of Jacobin nationalism and first-hand witness of its impact. 'It is so exclusive as to sacrifice everything to the public interest, without pity, without fear, without respect for humanity ... What produces the general good is always terrible.'[10] This nationalism, which admitted no more than the will of the majority, finally turned militant, aggressive and imperialist and became a threat to France's neighbours. Napoleon Bonaparte took it to the logical conclusion.

There is every justification for designating 'Jacobin' nationalism, which was first described by the American historian Carlton Hayes, as a specific type,[11] the early forerunner of integral nationalism. As a widespread political phenomenon, however, the latter is of far more recent date. There are good grounds for regarding integral nationalism as the offspring of the 'genuine' form of Risorgimento nationalism – hence the term 'derivative' nationalism. Integral nationalism can take root in any people, and it is possible roughly to indicate under what circumstances this may happen. The nation-state – the goal of Risorgimento nationalism – provides the framework for its development. In simple terms, integral nationalism is only possible in a world of established nation-states. It represents an aggressive ideology that asserts the interests of one nation-state in a ruthless and expansionist manner.

---

[10] Quoted in: Elie Kedourie, *Nationalism*, London 1961, p. 18.
[11] C. J. H. Hayes, *The Historical Evolution of Modern Nationalism* (1931), 8th ed., New York 1963.

4.1 The Roots of Integral Nationalism and its Organizational Forms

Historical and sociological analyses of nationalism often maintain that integral nationalism seems to have been a very prominent feature of the 'belated nations' (Helmuth Plessner) in the first half of the twentieth century. Germans, Italians, and, to some extent, the Japanese were inclined to regard themselves compared with older nation-states as disadvantaged competitors in the colonial race to divide up the world. Especially at a time when political and economic penetration into underdeveloped areas of the globe was being lauded as the great new national project, they attempted to compensate for their deficiencies which turned into a kind of collective inferiority complex, with an aggressive form of nationalism.

While it may be pertinent to point to the relevance of delays in the establishment of these national states, it would be equally misleading to restrict the phenomenon of integral nationalism to the special cases of Italian Fascism and German National Socialism. Taking as a point of departure its generic feature – the absoluteness of the nation – it is possible to arrive at a considerably broader spectrum of variations. We can thus say, for example, that from the 1880s onwards in Imperial Germany various pressure groups were committed to integral nationalism. The Pan-German League, formed in 1891 and surviving until 1939, whose spokesmen regarded national unification in 1871 as nothing more than a stepping stone for Germany to become a world power, was the most famous of what were known simply as 'national associations' (*nationale Verbände*) in this period. They also included the Association for Germandom Abroad (established in 1881), the German Colonial Society (1887–1936), the German Union of the Eastern Marches (1894–1935) and the German Navy League (1898–1934).[12]

The popular 'national associations' struck a chord in the hearts of the bourgeoisie of Imperial Germany, who shared many of their ideas and, indeed, identified with their aims. The leading historian Heinrich von Treitschke, for example, and the sociologist Max Weber, both of them representatives of the educated German middle classes, lent eloquent expression to the nation's bubbling vitality and missionary zeal and to Germany's changing political climate. As Treitschke wrote in 1884, the Reich, that 'young giant', should only employ its might 'for the purpose of improving the morality of humanity, and to render the name of Germany both fearsome and dear to the world', by 'playing its venerable part in the great task of extending civilization'. Max Weber, for his part, urged in 1895: 'We must grasp that the unification of Germany was a youthful spree, indulged in by the nation in its old age; it would have been better

[12] Hans-Ulrich Wehler, *The German Empire 1871–1918*, Leamington Spa 1985, pp. 83–90. Geoffrey Eley, *Reshaping the German Right. Radical Nationalism and Political Change after Bismarck*, New Haven 1980. *Idem*, 'The Wilhelmine Right: How it Changed', in: Richard J. Evans (ed.), *Society and Politics in Wilhelmine Germany*, London 1978, pp. 112–35. Marilyn Shevin Coetzee, *The German Army League. Popular Nationalism in Wilhelmine Germany*, Oxford 1990.

if it had never taken place, since it would have been a costly extravagance, if it was the conclusion rather than the starting-point for German power-politics on a global scale.'[13]

The 'national associations' launched their propaganda and action against the parliamentary order and Social Democracy, leaving a deep mark on the political system of Wilhelmine Germany. All the active associations, some of which, like the German Navy League, at times boasted as many as 80,000 individual and corporate members, shared a belief in an objective national interest that overrode, and was morally far superior to, party politics. As the self-appointed guardians of this national interest, they reserved for themselves the exclusive right to determine what it actually was. In this sense, the 'national associations' used nationalism as an ideology of integration and as an instrument that was as convenient as it was effective in cementing the political and social status quo. In Wilhelmine Germany, the existing order seemed to be at grave risk from the diverging interests of social groups, from the disconcerting side-effects of society's rapid and unbridled transition to developed industrialism after 1871, and from the rise of the socialist labour movement. In the minds of the 'national associations', however, the German nation would be impotent to compete with other nations, and incapable of extending the Reich throughout the world if it lacked steadfast internal cohesion and unity. Germany would be deprived of its 'place in the sun', as Bernhard von Bülow, who went on to become Reich Chancellor, expressed in 1897. A lever of 'negative integration' was operated in domestic and foreign policy, and images of a hostile world beyond Germany's borders were evoked to whip up support at home for the nationalist cause; ongoing political tensions with other countries were artificially heightened to bolster national loyalty.[14] In this way, nationalism transformed domestic friction and manoeuvring into dangerous conflicts between sovereign nations.

The emancipatory and liberal ambitions that lay at the very heart of Risorgimento nationalism were completely submerged by the 'national associations' which assigned to nationalist ideology an entirely new function. The liberal middle classes had once armed themselves with national slogans; now the slogans were being wielded against liberals and all hues on the Left. From the late 1870s, nobody opposed to reactionary politics could sympathize with nationalism, which, in the words of Golo Mann, now rang as an 'empty sound, serving only to nurture arrogance and to disguise and promote material enrichment.'[15] Even as Bismarck's days in power drew to an end, Ludwig Bamberger, a Liberal Reichstag deputy who was profoundly disturbed by the new imperial German nationalism,

---

[13] Heinrich von Treitschke, 'Die ersten Versuche deutscher Kolonialpolitik', in: *idem, Deutsche Kämpfe. Schriften zur Tagespolitik*, Leipzig 1896, p. 335. Max Weber, *Selections in Translation*, ed. by W. G. Runciman and E. Matthews, Cambridge 1978, p. 266.

[14] Dieter Groh, *Negative Integration und revolutionärer Attentismus. Die deutsche Sozialdemokratie am Vorabend des Ersten Weltkrieges*, Frankfurt 1973. Wehler, *The German Empire*, pp. 90–4 and 102–105.

[15] Golo Mann, *The History of Germany since 1789*, reprint Harmondsworth 1985, p. 462.

commented that 'a generation [has] emerged ... for whom patriotism signifies hatred; a hatred of everything both at home and abroad that refuses unquestioningly to go down on its knees.'[16]

Yet the intellectual proximity between nationalism and right-wing radicalism was not unique to Germany in the late nineteenth and early twentieth centuries. Similar things could be found in Britain too, where the Navy League, for example, founded in 1894, doubted that the stability of British society could be maintained in an age when trade unions were being legalized and the electoral system comprehensively reformed.[17] Other prominent organizations to subscribe to these views included the National Service League, created in 1902, and the Imperial Maritime League of 1907. A philosophy of imperialism; notions of a 'Greater' Britain; belief in the superiority of the British political and social system; anti-Semitism, whose power is all too easily underestimated; demands for protectionist policies to fend off foreign economic competition: these were the ingredients of an aggressive British nationalism that became known at the time as jingoism. The Boer War of 1898–1901 in South Africa and the naval rivalry between Britain and Germany that broke out after the turn of the century, were the effective catalysts in the formation of a 'radical Right' which urged that imperial policy should serve the 'national interest' of Britain alone, and that the Empire be built up into a kind of closely-knit 'super-state'.

The marriage between nationalism and imperialism, between the might of the national state and overseas colonial expansion, was celebrated in Italy too. This happened, indeed, long before Mussolini embarked upon a strident policy of annexation and adopted 'mare nostro' as a motto that now referred not merely to the Adriatic, but to the entire Mediterranean. In the eyes of the early Italian nationalists, the process of national unification that had begun in 1859 with the war between Austria and Piedmont, was completed when Rome was taken in September 1870 and became the capital of Italy. But many Italians still lived beyond the borders of the national state of 1870: in the Austrian Trentino, and in the city and surrounding areas of Trieste they outnumbered German Austrians and Slovenes; substantial Italian minorities lived in Istria, in Dalmatia, which had been under Venitian rule from 1420 to 1797, and in South Tyrol; Ticino was a Swiss canton, while Nice and Corsica were French. From the late nineteenth century onwards, expansionist Italian nationalism was organized in such bodies as the Società Dante Alighieri, the Lega Navale, the Società Geografica, and then after 1910 in the Associazione Nazionalista Italiana. They felt that major Italian areas 'yet to be redeemed' were in the hands of the Habsburg monarchy. This could only mean that such regions also had to be incorporated into the Italian nation-state, by force if necessary, irrespective of the fact that they were inhabited by various numbers of non-Italians too. The most dubious of historical arguments

---

[16] Ludwig Bamberger, *Die Nachfolge Bismarcks*, 2nd ed., Berlin 1889, p. 41.

[17] Anne Summers, 'The Character of Edwardian Nationalism: Three Popular Leagues', in: Paul Kennedy/Anthony J. Nicholls (eds), *Nationalist and Racialist Movements in Britain and Germany before 1914*, London 1981, p. 75.

were concocted to reinforce Italian ambitions, with the demagogic cry of 'Italia irredenta' (unredeemed Italy) first being raised in 1877.

Though costly and the cause of heavy losses, Italy's colonial adventures in Africa were greeted with much enthusiasm by the nationalists. In the decade before the First World War, a period when Italy was undergoing rapid industrialization together with all the accompanying social convulsions, expansionists almost fell over themselves developing programme after programme of colonial action. But these turned out to be largely impractical. After the war against Ottoman Turkey in 1911–12, Italian nationalism was able to chalk up colonial gains in the shape of Libya and the Dodecanese Islands in the Aegean. The Treaty of London signed in April 1915 promised Italy sizeable territorial gains on its northern borders if she entered the war on the side of the Allies. Victory over the central powers would bring her not only the Austrian Trentino and Trieste, but also the Tyrol up to the Brenner Pass, Istria, and large parts of Dalmatia. By supporting these expansionist policies, Sidney Sonnino, then Italy's Foreign Minister, followed a course diametrically opposed to the liberalism at the core of the Risorgimento movement and to Mazzini's ideals, which had prescribed Italy the role of protector, not oppressor, of the southern Slavs. Italy was now riding roughshod over the rights and freedom of other peoples. When the war was over, Italy in fact gained less than promised in 1915, mainly due to American resistance at the Paris Peace Conference. Nevertheless, simply because their neighbours, members of the Italian nation, touted extremist nationalism in 1919, no fewer than 250,000 Germans in South Tyrol, and more than 500,000 Croats and Slovenes were denied the right of self-determination that President Wilson had so ardently defended. But even this did not satisfy the Italian nationalists: the Paris Peace Treaties they felt, sealed the 'lost victory' because areas inhabited by Italian minorities were included in the new southern Slavic state, which in 1929 became Yugoslavia.

Disappointment over the outcome of the Great War pained many Italians and provided the fertile breeding ground for fascism, which came to power as early as 27–28 October 1922, with Mussolini's 'march on Rome', initiating the replacement of parliamentary democracy by the totalitarian state. Prior to this, the Partito Nazionale Fascista had been founded in 1921 and went on to become the first party in Europe to win mass support for a programme of right-wing nationalism. Before 1918, political parties in Europe espousing extremist nationalism heavily tinged with anti-Semitism had managed to gain no more than passing favour. Such a fate befell, for example, the German 'Nationals' around the landowner Georg von Schönerer in Austria, and the Christian Social Party in Germany, founded in 1889 by the demagogic Berlin court chaplain Adolf Stoecker, which substituted the Jews as the enemy within for the enemy without.

By contrast, many parts of post-war Europe saw the emergence in the 1920s and 1930s of fascist parties and authoritarian movements, most of them modelled on Italian lines, whose extreme nationalism advocated a radical transformation of the existing state and society. They portrayed themselves as the saviours of the nation from the threat posed both by socialism and the labour movement, as well as by international capitalism and liberalism. These radical, anti-bourgeois, anti-liberal and anti-Marxist organizations, which cropped up under a whole range of names, included the National Socialist Workers' Party in Germany (founded in 1919–20), the Heimwehren (Home Defence Units) in Austria (1918), the Rex in Belgium (1930), the Iron Guard in Romania (1930), the Nationaal Socialistische Beweging in the Netherlands (1931), the Nasjonal Samling in Norway (1933), Oswald Mosley's Black Shirts in Britain (1933), the Falange in Spain (1934), and the Parti Populaire Français in France (1936). The mainstay of fascism in all its varieties was provided by the old and new middle classes. Faced with the growth of the labour movement and the march of industrialization, artisans, retailers, white-collar workers, civil servants and farmers felt their material existence and social status to be under threat. Their anxieties and hopes made them receptive to anti-Semitism and forms of integral nationalism.

4.2 Integral Nationalism and the Political Environment

In an attempt to explain the political and social circumstances under which the integral nationalism that characterized post-1918 fascist parties and movements could arise, Eugen Lemberg has offered the thesis that the crystallization of such extreme sentiments is generally preceded by a crisis of national self-confidence, the putative looming of extraordinary perils from outside, real or perceived threats to the continued existence of the nation. In Lemberg's view, this happens in particular when a nation has suffered a crushing military or political defeat injurious to its collective sense of self-esteem and conducive to a situation in which the integrative forces needed for future survival of the nation begin to weaken. Perceiving the supposed danger of disintegration, the nation, regarded by Lemberg as a collective individual, embraces a form of integral nationalism.[18]

Lemberg offers two examples to underpin his case: French nationalism in the decades following military defeat in the Franco-German war of 1870–71; and German nationalism after 1918. Neither people could cope with defeats they experienced as serious blemishes upon their pride and respective national histories. The French responded by embarking upon a mission to civilize the world that eventually led to cultural nationalism and imperialism overseas. The writer and politician Paul Déroulède, who formed the League of Patriots in 1882, urged the nation to contemplate its fate and safeguard its unity, which had been shaken not least by the growing strength of the French labour movement. He espoused the idea that the humbled French nation should remember its historical greatness. This was but one step short of demanding the purification of a 'degenerate' nation swamped by foreigners, a battle cry for hunting down a scapegoat for the country's critical collapse in 1870. The political climate in France, rife as it was with suspicion and incrimination, allowed the racial doctrine conceived long before by Comte de Gobineau to achieve considerable

---

[18] Eugen Lemberg, *Nationalismus*, vol. 1, Reinbek 1964, pp. 198–203.

popularity. In conjunction with Edouard Drumont's work *La France juive* ('Jewish France'), published in 1886, it formed the basis for widespread anti-Semitism which erupted in spectacular fashion with the Dreyfus affair in 1894–1900, deepening the divisions of French society even further. As the episode reached its high-point in 1898, Action française, a radical right-wing organization headed by Charles Maurras, emerged, placing the entire blame for France's putative political and moral decline firmly and squarely on the shoulders of parliamentarianism, liberalism, internationalism and Jewry. The explosive mix of irrationality and demagogy exercised a fascination over the French that went far beyond the ranks of the Action française. If we examine the symbols and slogans, the passion and hatred aroused in battles against political opponents, and the loathing of democracy, we can justifiably say that the Action française was a forerunner of fascism. But in countries like France, where there was a long tradition of revolution and democracy, integral nationalism failed to dominate entirely and to distort society, for the liberal bourgeoisie provided an effective counterweight. This was not the case in Germany.

In Germany after 1918, an integral nationalism rose and promised to purge, rejuvenate and redeem the nation as it had done in France after 1871. An immediate reaction to military defeat in the Great War and the 'dictat of Versailles' was the flourishing of a myth that Germany had suffered a 'stab in the back'. Within a few months the legend was to become a 'mainstay of the conservative-nationalist ideology of self-justification and aggression'.[19] The burden of guilt for the collapse of time-honoured values and for the country's current plight had to be placed on someone. At the same time, a constructive way out had to be found through achievements in science and culture as well as through a show of national unity. As the saying went after 1918, the war was lost by the monarchical system, not the people; faith in the nation would be the source of energy and inspiration for Germany to rise to glory again. Never was so much written and talked about the German cultural mission, or so much effort made to distinguish between German *Kultur* and French *civilisation*, as during the turbulent years immediately following the First World War. And never was there a louder, more persistent cry to be heard in Germany for strong leadership, for a mighty man who would reunite the torn *Volk* and lead it from the bondage of the 'shameful peace' of Versailles to new heights.

Integral nationalism in both France and Germany was nurtured by the stinging shock of military defeat. Nazi Germany was to take it to unprecedented extremes. Eugen Lemberg takes the exceptional situations in which France and Germany found themselves to be crises of national self-confidence. Yet the political histories of Imperial Germany, France, Britain or Italy from the late nineteenth century onwards make clear that we should expand Lemberg's thesis concerning the circumstances under which integral nationalism was likely to arise. It should include the systemic economic and social crises that inevitably ensued after industrialization

---

[19] Eberhard Kolb, *The Weimar Republic*, London 1988, p. 35.

and with the rise of the labour movement. In mass industrialized society, nationalism, which by this stage at the latest has become highly flexible, serves as a psychological release valve for the kind of political and social pressure that mounted in Germany and other countries during the so-called Great Depression between 1873 and 1896, a period of severe slumps and a worldwide slow-down in economic growth. Its task is to divert attention from social unrest and domestic conflicts. Conservative power élites consciously exploit the emotional vulnerability of a society that has been subjected to fundamental change. In their hands, nationalism becomes a dangerous, though only superficially effective instrument of crisis management and maintenance of power. As a 'technique of domination' that is especially good at rallying the bourgeois classes behind the traditional élites in times of convulsive trauma, nationalism may be able, at least temporarily, to quell crises at home. But this is usually only possible at the cost of creating tension with neighbours and serious predicaments abroad.

It is comparatively easy to distinguish between Risorgimento nationalism and integral nationalism as generic types because of their substantive differences and because the latter can be more readily manipulated. Carlton Hayes has gone so far as to use 'counter nationalism' when speaking about integral nationalism: the terms 'conservative' and 'national' become practically synonymous here, while in Risorgimento nationalism they are antonyms. Liberal Risorgimento nationalism arises under conditions and in contexts that are quite different from those obtaining in the case of integral nationalism. However, both types are in more than one respect the products of crises: crises of political participation and the regulation of social power; of conflicts generated by the modernization of social infrastructure and political institutions; of economic development and the distribution of national income. In its pure form, integral nationalism is a relative latecomer in the history of modern nationalism since the French Revolution. In many cases it is even possible to pinpoint the juncture at which the switch from 'genuine' to 'derivative', from 'left-wing' to 'right-wing' nationalism took place. With the creation of the nation-state, Risorgimento nationalism had reached its goal, and in purely functional terms became obsolete; what followed was no more than a sentimental epilogue. In the nation-state, it lived on as a retrospective ideology glorifying in what it had achieved, consolidating and maintaining national consciousness, and acting as an agent in the ongoing process of nation-building. This type of nationalism is, in both everyday and academic language, a 'normal' and legitimate phenomenon, often termed 'traditional' or 'healthy' nationalism. In Germany after 1871, 'traditional' nationalism, which does not define the 'nation' as the sacred repository of all values, came to refer to the nation comprising the *kleindeutsch*, or 'lesser' German state.

The history of Europe, however, shows that as soon as the national movements which battled for political freedom and self-determination had gained victory, the solidarity they had shown towards each other began to crumble. Erstwhile fraternal revolutionaries warring against the status quo rapidly changed into national egotists. Mazzini's idealistic hopes for a more peaceful world order were dashed; the *risorgimento* image of the world, to which he had given classic literary expression, turned out to be a utopia. It proved impossible to harmonize the interests of peoples whose emancipation and freedom had been the clarion call of Risorgimento nationalism.

The new system of nation-states which emerged from the early nineteenth century onwards was as incapable of guaranteeing a peaceful world order as the order it had replaced. Instead, the nation-state served to delineate a framework within which emancipatory and 'legitimate' nationalism metamorphosed into the conservative, indeed reactionary ideology of integration that represents nationalism as it is normally understood today. This form of nationalism, whose ultimate goal seems to be to mobilize those parts of society constituting the 'nation' to protect the domestic status quo against internal and external enemies, tends, unfairly, to obscure the earlier movements for national independence that emerged in Europe in the nineteenth and twentieth centuries. Historical experience over two centuries has shown this if nothing else: the undeniable transformation that nationalism undergoes from a rather progressive 'left-wing' body of thought into a predominantly 'right-wing' ideology of integration. As such it is opposed to cosmopolitanism, internationalism, liberalism and socialism. Integral nationalism is not the inevitable consequence of Risorgimento nationalism or any other form of nationalism apostrophized as 'legitimate' that might precede it; neither does this development in different nations exhibit the same pattern, time scale or intensity. The possibility of this happening is, however, present in every society that conceives of itself as a nation. The specific political and social context determines whether, and in which way, integral nationalism might evolve.

5 National Socialism in Germany

The reasons why integral nationalism happened to take on such unique proportions in Germany have been exhaustively discussed elsewhere. We shall not cover the same ground in detail again, nor re-examine the history of National Socialism before and after January 1933. Instead, the focus will be on two closely related features of integral nationalism in Germany which distinguish it from comparable cases of this type of nationalism in other countries: first, its dominant ideational representation of geopolitical space, which burst the boundaries of the national state founded in 1871; and secondly its specific policies of *Volk* and race. Expansionism in foreign policy was justified by the simple pretext of having to acquire more 'living space' (*Lebensraum*) for the German people and assert Germany's power on the world stage. The thoroughly systematic application of Nazism's racial ideology, which derived from a crude social Darwinism, led to the most hideous crimes. In particular, National Socialism elevated the *Volk* – the organic community founded upon common origin, language and culture and in existence independently of institutional political boundaries – to an absolute value unfettered by any restriction whatsoever, and crushing all ethical and moral obstacles that happened to stand in its path.

One of the roots of the National Socialist hybrid of integral nationalism lay in the *völkisch* nationalism of the Weimar Republic. This type of nationalism, the first signs of which can be traced back to Imperial Germany, referred not only to the *kleindeutsch* nation of 1871, but as a matter of principle to all Germans wherever they lived. German *Volkstum* – German folkdom or national heritage – was perceived as the invigorating source for the renewal of a greater German Reich, and became a key concept for conservative intellectuals.[20]

German Austrians had been forbidden union with the rest of Germany by the Versailles Treaty, and after 1918 German minorities were assigned to foreign states, some of which were entirely new creations. The prime concern of the ideologues of *völkisch* nationalism was consequently to maintain and strengthen the German way of life both in the Reich and in the diaspora. Various pressure groups and institutions, largely independent of the Berlin government, turned their attention in particular to the pockets of German-language speakers and the *Volksgruppen*, or groups of ethnic Germans, as they were then called, residing in East-Central and South-East Europe. These included the Association for Germandom Abroad, which had emerged from the General German School Association in 1908, the Institute for Frontier and Foreign Studies, founded in Berlin in 1920, and the German Foreign Institute, established in Stuttgart in 1917. They were motivated by hopes of a new German Empire which would heal the wounds of the disintegrating nation, re-incorporate those sections of the people segregated off in East-Central Europe, and effectively protect the ethnic German communities (*Volksgruppen*) abroad. The contours of the future 'Third Reich', a catchword coined by the writer Arthur Moeller van den Bruck in 1923, were still hazy; but this in all likelihood is the very reason why the concept was so fascinating. For the 'Third Reich' was clearly not the Reich described in the democratic constitution of the Weimar Republic, but, rather, an authoritarian *grossdeutsch* Reich including Austria: probably a Reich that in some way formed a continuation of the universalist German Reich of medieval times.

Along with most exponents of *völkisch* nationalism, Hitler felt that in practice the often-evoked Third Reich, which from 1938 he threatened forcibly to create, would have little to do with the idea of the German national state that had held good since the nineteenth century. His major aim was not to finish building the German nation-state, but to bring 'our territorial area into just proportion with the number of our population'.[21] This opened the floodgates for a sweeping policy of annexation, and led him ruthlessly to subordinate the claims of other 'inferior' races to the unbridled ambition of the German people for 'living space' in the east.

---

[20] Armin Mohler, *Die konservative Revolution in Deutschland 1918–1932*, Stuttgart 1950. Warren B. Morris, *The Weimar Republic and Nazi Germany*, Chicago 1982. Michael Hughes, *Nationalism and Society. Germany 1800–1945*, London 1988, pp. 189–205. Edgar J. Feuchtwanger, *From Weimar to Hitler. Germany 1918–33*, London 1993.

[21] Adolf Hitler, *Mein Kampf*, transl. by J. Murphy, London n.d., p. 552. Louis L. Snyder, 'The Nationalism of Adolf Hitler', in: *idem, Roots of German Nationalism*, Bloomington (Ind.)/London 1978, pp. 188–216.

Hitler and other representatives of the Nazi regime patently envisaged a thorough revision of the European order in Germany's favour, along with a broad process of Germanization that would steamroller over areas where other peoples and minorities had historically settled. As far as can be gathered from the often contradictory and vague statements of National Socialist politicians, the voracious and hegemonial 'Germanic Reich of the German Nation', which increasingly seized hold of Hitler's imagination after Austria and the Sudetenland had been annexed in 1938, was eventually to incorporate western Germanic peoples like the Alsatians, Luxembourgers, Flemings and Dutch, and in Northern Europe to attach to itself the Scandinavian peoples in satellite states. The first country to be engulfed by the 'Great Germanic Reich' was Luxembourg in August 1942. In Eastern Europe, the Reich would extend its territory substantially, and in so doing, 'without further ado remove [alien racial elements] and hand over the vacated territory to its own national comrades'.[22]

Hitler had thus spoken as early as 1928. In other words, when the Nazis began to strip the peoples of Eastern Europe of their rights, drive them from their traditional homelands, brutally deprive them of their nationality, and, finally, perpetrate genocide on Poles, Ukrainians, Jews and others, the theoretical foundations of their monstrous actions had been spelled out long before. Just a few days after the Polish campaign of autumn 1939 the regime had started systematically to implement its criminal policy towards East-Central and Eastern Europe, which amounted to 'ethnic-national reclamation of land' or, in modern terms, to 'ethnic cleansing'. In terms of its sheer size and the cold-blooded cruelty with which it was executed, it outdid anything that Europe had ever witnessed until then. Even fanatical defenders of the principle of nationality had not dreamed such things could happen. Though everyone talked of the national heritage policy and the cult of the folk, the Nazi programme represented its 'utter negation'.[23] In October 1939, the notorious Heinrich Himmler was appointed 'Reich Commissar for the Strengthening of Germandom'. His brief was forcibly to resettle the German nationals living scattered in various parts of Eastern and South-Eastern Europe either in the core German state that had been enlarged through annexation, or in conquered and occupied territory. The Reich Commissariats planned for these areas to act as 'overseas' settler colonies and to supply the mainland 'Great Germanic Reich' with raw materials and foodstuff.

In its totality this was a concept that scrupulously disregarded historically evolved circumstances, scorned every humanitarian consideration, and pushed the ethnic German communities from one place to the next in the interests of a crazed scheme of world domination. Estimates put the number of German nationals caught up in this resettlement programme

---

[22] Thus Hitler. See *Hitler's Secret Book*. Introduction by Telford Taylor, New York 1961, pp. 47–48.

[23] Ernst Ritter, *Das Deutsche Ausland-Institut in Stuttgart 1917–1945. Ein Beispiel deutscher Volkstumsarbeit zwischen den Weltkriegen*, Wiesbaden 1976, p. 136. Louis L. Snyder, 'Nationalism in the Third Reich', in: *idem, Roots of German Nationalism*, pp. 217–36.

of the Nazis at almost one million.[24] The way in which the South Tyroleans were treated, the only German *Volksgruppe* living in an area bordering directly on German-speaking territory, illustrates how Nazi power at home and abroad was so calculating, ruthless and manipulative. According to the terms of an agreement concluded with Mussolini's Italy, Germany's ally since 1936, those who opted for Germany could move to the Reich. Between 1939 and 1942, 75,000 South Tyroleans left their homes.[25] In 1942, Hitler temporarily entertained the idea of resettling the South Tyroleans in the Crimea, where he had yet to create the *Reichsgau Taurien*, but the monstrous idea never left the drawing board.

Resettlement of whole groups of people represented nothing short of the heedless manipulation of human beings. It reached its high-point in 1940, but three years later was disrupted by military developments in the European theatre. Dogmatic faith in the alleged superiority of the German people and the Germanic race had led Hitler and the Nazi leadership permanently to overestimate their power. When Germans began to be driven out of East-Central Europe and the German areas east of the rivers Oder and Neisse from late 1944, the plot the Nazis had in their blindness conceived and put into practice unexpectedly backfired. The racist imperialism of the Third Reich and its war of ethnic extermination turned into the 'German catastrophe', as Friedrich Meinecke put it. But it was Europe's catastrophe too.

---

[24] Theodor Schieder, 'Europa im Zeitalter der Weltmächte', in: *idem* (ed.), *Handbuch der Europäischen Geschichte*, Stuttgart 1979, vol. 7, p. 9.
[25] Felix Ermacora, *Südtirol und das Vaterland Österreich*, Vienna 1984, p. 33.

3

Risorgimento Nationalism in Europe

I Nationalism in the Age of the French Revolution

It is relatively easy to pinpoint the rise in a society of integral nationalism. But what about its earlier Risorgimento counterpart? From which point is it possible to say that any kind of nationalism exists? These questions are still or, rather, once again the subject of much controversy among historians and social scientists. A good case can be presented to support the relatively widely held opinion that the great European nations – the 'historic' nations – were already taking shape in the early Middle Ages. But it proves quite impossible to say exactly when the process of nation-building set in. Hard evidence of national feeling and thought, of an awareness of national differences and national identity, dating from the medieval and early modern periods is not difficult to locate; but it is inaccurate to say that nationalism existed even in those times, let alone to claim, as some have done, that the ancient world knew a Jewish or Greek nationalism.[1] French, English, Italian or Spanish consciousness of individuality dating from the Middle Ages remained embedded as much in traditional Christian universalism as in historically evolved close regional and corporate relations.

Received opinion holds that nationalism in the modern sense does not date back further than the revolutionary political turmoil that troubled the second half of the eighteenth century. It was born in France. French national consciousness after 1789 was novel because it was, first, purely secular and, secondly, both an expression and instrument of mass political mobilization. Thus ever since the French Revolution, nationalism has been understood as an ideology and a political movement borne by broad sections of society which declares emotional attachment to the nation to be the supreme bond and whose goal is self-determination for the nation in a national state. Modern nationalism after 1789 has a programme for a new political and social reality, and is organized. As a reflection of this, the term often used by medieval authors – *natio* – does not mean the same as *nation* after 1789. The post-revolutionary world sees the nation as an agency imparting a binding meaning to the order of things and acting as

---

[1] E. D. Marcu, *Sixteenth-Century Nationalism*, New York 1976. C. L. Tipton (ed.), *Nationalism in the Middle Ages*, New York 1972.

a source of justification for thought and deed. By contrast, the meaning of *natio*, deriving from the Latin *nasci*, to be born, is far narrower, and relates to people of common background and origin, to areas of settlement, to geographical settings and their inhabitants; but not to a political formation. The 'Nation' in the Holy Roman Empire of the German Nation referred solely to the German-speaking aristocracy as the ruling strata in that supra-national organization of states. When the Empire concluded the Peace of Szátmar with the 'Hungarian nation' in 1711, it was not with the people as a totality but with the 'barons, prelates and aristocrats of Hungary'. The socially privileged classes in Hungary and Poland constituted an 'aristocratic nation'. National consciousness and the modern nation thus have a long pedigree, whereas nationalism as an ideology and a political movement does not; modern nationalism is a child of the French, and to some degree also of the American, Revolution.

In the Great Revolution of 1789, the inhabitants of the provinces ruled by the French king transcended regional, corporate and religious barriers and joined together as the people of a state, as a political nation. As the new central community the nation was not supposed completely to iron out these differences, but to build a lasting bridge between them and put an end to their divisive nature. When asked in 1789 what a nation was, Abbé Sieyès remarked that it was a 'body of associates living under one common law and represented by the same legislature.[2] The political and social community of equal citizens wished to decide its own destiny, to become the subject, not the object, of political will. 'Nation' was the battle cry that the revolutionaries raised against feudal society, thereby destroying the basis on which rule had traditionally been legitimated. The revolutionary concept of society was that of a community of all politically conscious and equal citizens. This community was now the source of legitimacy for the state and the exercise of rule; the nation was, from now on, the sole repository of power. The bourgeoisie rose to lead the people by claiming control of state power. In Sieyès's classic formulation, the Third Estate had become the 'universal' class and identified itself with the nation. As the dominant intellectual and economic force, its task was to rise to political leadership and complete the transformation of the body of feudally organized, immature subjects into a society of responsible citizens.

Armed with a concept of the nation that revolved round freedom and equality, the revolutionary movement was initially opposed to internal enemies, composed first and foremost of the old ruling élite of the aristocracy together with the clergy, both of which had entirely forfeited their authority. Insofar as they failed to join the revolutionary bourgeoisie, the hitherto privileged strata were deemed to be excluded from the nation. In the next phase of development, French nationalism began to turn against the monarchical governments of Europe, the vehemence with which it did so depending on how energetically the various *anciens régimes* disputed the sovereignty of the French nation and the legitimacy of its newly created

---

[2] Quoted in: Elie Kedourie, *Nationalism*, London 1961, p. 15.

political order. In France, the outbreak of war against the hostile European monarchies in 1792 inspired the idea that other peoples should be led along the path to the liberty wrested by the revolution: the French nation had acquired a mission.

The model of revolutionary social and political transformation was much admired outside France too. The demand for political responsibility which, as a community of politically aware citizens, the French bourgeoisie raised, was being addressed ever more vociferously to princes, kings and the traditional power élites all over Europe. On a different level, the domination of Europe, to which the Napoleonic motherland of the revolution aspired with considerable success, also fanned a spirit of resistance among those who found they were being denied the very freedom and self-determination that the *grande nation* was proclaiming from the rooftops of Europe as the fruits of 1789. Ultimately, French expansionism and ambitions to rule supreme led monarchical governments in Central Europe to appeal to the patriotism of their subjects to help repel the French drive for political hegemony.

The paradoxical nature of this constellation of forces is most clearly illustrated by the political situation in Germany at the beginning of the nineteenth century. On the one hand, early German nationalism took its cue from revolutionary France and the ideas of human and civil rights, democracy and popular sovereignty propagated there. Yet owing to Napoleon's expansionist policies, German Risorgimento nationalism was also coloured by tangibly anti-French sentiments. Revolutionary ideas about the equality of all and the sovereignty of the people go most of the way in explaining why nationalism in Germany too was directed against both internal and external enemies. The rising middle classes saw themselves as the natural agents of the nation, understood as a cultural community, and as the engine of its political unity. The bourgeoisie would only be able to realize its full economic and political potential in a German national state; the entrenched dynasties and aristocracies in the existing plethora of German states were blocking the way. Consequently, early German nationalism was anti-feudal and anti-dynastic, though only inasmuch as individual states, and especially Prussia, the largest and most powerful, did not take up the cause of German unification. Nationalism equated with opposition to the domestic status quo, to monarchical authority, to the particularism of the individual German states, and to the arbitrary denial of political freedoms. Theories on how far these freedoms should go, and what their nature should be, had long since been in circulation. Finally, German nationalism, at least in its early stages, also equated with resolute opposition to French domination of Central Europe.

2 The 'National Awakening' of the European Peoples

In Germany the intriguing ideas of the French Revolution, Herder's philosophy, and the immediate experience of foreign rule were the foundation stones for a political movement that recognized the self-determining nation as the sole source of legitimate government and the sovereign nation-state as the proper form of political organization. The critical watershed in German political thought occurred at the turn of the eighteenth and nineteenth centuries. It was a process whose form and development were strikingly similar among other European peoples, particularly the so-called 'unhistorical' peoples in the east and south-east of the continent. This was a more or less European-wide happening that proceeded like a chain-reaction from the early nineteenth century onwards. The links in the chain shared common circumstances, and were mutually influential. In the consciousness of the east and south-east European peoples, the exciting process marked a decisive turning-point in their existence: it heralded a New Beginning against which everything that had happened before would pale into insignificance. Prince Ypsilantis' seal, for instance, showed a phoenix above the flames, and it was occasionally suggested that the phoenix be incorporated into the emblem of the new Greek national polity to symbolize the 'rebirth' of the state, the coming of age of the nation.

The peoples of Europe also gave similar names to the development which conceived humanity as a society of politically autonomous cultural communities. They spoke of the rise of the nation, national awakening, national rebirth and so on. The Italians called it *risorgimento* (resurrection) after the journal *Il Risorgimento*, published from the end of 1847 by Cesare Balbo in the Piedmontese capital of Turin. In the journal's early days, one of its major contributors was Cavour, one of the great pioneers of Italian unification and after 1852 the dynamic prime minister of the Kingdom of Piedmont and Sardinia. Scholars of nationalism have adopted the term Risorgimento as a generic description of emancipatory nationalism because its core meaning is so appropriate.

The 'national awakening' of European peoples which began in the early nineteenth century was a collective process in which the role of the 'awakeners' was crucial. Since then, every nation has done its utmost to praise the deeds and merits of the philologists, poets, historians and politicians who substantiated, and in most cases successfully asserted the nation's claim to independence and self-determination. In the words of the philosopher Friedrich Schleiermacher, alongside the founders and 'purifiers of religions', these 'makers and recreators of states' were 'great men', individuals powerful enough to have wrought the shape of history.[3] The German national movement counted among its 'awakeners' Johann Gottfried Herder, the philosopher Johann Gottlieb Fichte, who roused Germans to national rejuvenation in his 'Addresses to the German Nation' in the winter of 1807–1808, Friedrich Ludwig Jahn, the 'father of gymnastics', and the journalist Ernst Moritz Arndt. The Greeks cite the writer Rhigas Velestinlis and the great philologist and linguistic innovator Adamantios Korais, who spent almost his entire life abroad and still managed to make an impact on his homeland. The Irish boast Daniel O'Connell, the 'liberator' and stirring public orator, and the writer Thomas Davis. The Poles, meanwhile, invoke the names of the historian Joachim Lelewel and the visionary poet Adam Mickiewicz, who proclaimed the

---

[3] *Schleiermachers Werke*, ed. by A. Dorner and O. Braun, Leipzig 1910, vol. 1, p. 529.

Polish nation's humanitarian messianism. His great work, *Pan Tadeusz*, became the Poles' national epic. The Czechs turn to the historian František Palacký, and to the East Prussian Herder for his famous chapter on the Slavs in his *Outlines of a Philosophy of the History of Man* (1791).[4]

The 'awakeners' generally proceeded from the assumption that the existence of a nation was a function of a shared language, and that linguistic uniformity was the precondition of a nation-state: a 'national language' was spoken in a national state, and linguistic frontiers were therefore the natural frontiers of states. In 1813 Ernst Moritz Arndt expressed a wish to see the 'whole of Germany' united 'as far and as wide as the German tongue is heard'. The importance of language as a criterion of cultural and political differentiation thus grew tremendously. It became a kind of status symbol almost everywhere, the object of a whole variety of scholarly and literary enterprises. More often than not, explicit reference was made to Herder, who had emphasized the intrinsic value of each language, since, he argued, all languages were equal before God, and the native tongue was the only one through which a human being could experience self-realization. Language was the external, visible element of all the features which drew the line between one nation and the next; it was the touchstone of whether a nation actually existed and was entitled to its own national state.

In many ways, the 'awakeners' were active creators of language. They established a literature in the national language, which itself had to be refashioned for literary and colloquial communication. Often as a result of the policies of discrimination and uniformity pursued by autocratic governments in multinational empires, many of these languages had long since ceased to be the everyday language of academics or the language of instruction in schools. In the case of Czech, Slovak, Flemish and Romanian, for example, the putatively 'national' language only existed as a peasant dialect. In the nineteenth-century Spanish theatre, Catalan was used to produce comic effects.

Linguistic movements could become the core of a radical nationalism disposed to the use of violence, particularly where the language of the people or a minority was subject to discrimination by a dominant 'official language' or high form (*Hochsprache*). This happened in the case of Catalan, Gaelic-Irish, Flemish and Basque. In many European states, the crystallization of nations was accompanied by battles over language: over the relationship between official and popular languages; over which should be the language of law and instruction; over which language government and administration should use; over which should be the language of command in the armed forces. The comparative validity of different tongues was at stake here.

Worse still, a few Baltic languages had not even achieved the status of languages of letters and literature, and educated people were consequently extremely reluctant to accept them as 'national' languages. In some cases the difficulties were so great as to thwart even whole movements fighting

---

[4] *Herders Sämtliche Werke*, ed. by Bernhard Suphan, Berlin 1909, vol. 14, pp. 277–78.

for the rejuvenation of a particular tongue. A perhaps extreme example from the history of European Risorgimento nationalism is that of Irish, which during the course of the nineteenth century was almost entirely displaced by English, the language of instruction in Irish schools since the middle part of that century. By the time the movement for the revival of Irish had emerged, Gaelic was only being spoken in the remote regions of west and south-west Ireland, the Gaeltacht. According to official records, it was used as the medium of day-to-day communication by no more than 14 per cent of the population in around 1891. This figure gives only a partial picture of the speed with which English had subjugated the indigenous vernacular since the mid-eighteenth century. Karl Marx may have had Irish in mind when he opined that the progressive development of civilization would cause peoples to abandon 'useless' languages. Despite the many efforts made particularly by the Gaelic League, founded in 1893, and then by the Irish Free State after 1922, to reintroduce Irish as an every-day language, English has to this day been able to shake off all challenges to the dominance it acquired in the nineteenth century. The Irish constitution credits English as 'a second official language' besides Irish, the 'first official language';[5] but this is more wishful nationalist thinking than anything else.

If political circumstances allowed, the 'awakeners' established learned societies, institutes and academies for the purposes of reviving, purifying and standardizing language; they made provision for the writing of grammars, dictionaries and anthologies; in some cases they even went so far as to forge manuscripts in order to prove that lost traditions of language and literature had once existed. The dilapidated 'national' language was to be refurbished to modern requirements by coinage and borrowing from related tongues. The frequent result was that the resuscitated standardized variety of the language acquired a learned and bookish flavour that clearly distinguished it from the language commonly spoken by the mass of the people. Greek and Norwegian, for example, developed two parallel varieties until a second wave of linguistic revivalism finally endowed the vernacular (dimotiki and landsmål) with literary status too. It was not until this point that the Greek and Norwegian nation-states possessed genuinely national languages. The Czech language movement had been demanding equal status for Czech and German in Bohemia, part of the Habsburg monarchy, as early as the revolutionary year of 1848; in 1882 it forced the bifurcation of Prague University into a German-speaking and a Czech-speaking school. The philosopher Thomas G. Masaryk, who was to become the first president of Czechoslovakia in 1918, lectured at the Czech university, which by 1907–08 had risen to be the second largest seat of learning in the Habsburg Empire after Vienna. 1890 witnessed the establishment in Prague of a Czech Academy of Arts and Sciences to coexist with the Royal Bohemian Society of Sciences that had been created in 1790.

Historians joined philologists and poets to play an important role in

---

[5] Article 8, *Bunreacht na hEireann. Constitution of Ireland*, Dublin 1951.

'national awakening'. They regarded as one of their most noble tasks the discovery of the nation's shared intellectual, cultural and political heritage, which would promote a sense of identity. In Germany Baron vom Stein steered through publication from 1819 onwards the *Monumenta Germaniae Historica*, a great collection of sources of medieval German history, to inspire interest in the nation's past. Each volume bore the motto *Sanctus amor patriae dat animum* ('holy love of the fatherland inspires us'). Similar enterprises were launched in other countries. Historiography, in John Pocock's phrase, was 'both the instrument and the record' of nation-building.[6]

Historians lent vitality to everything that apparently derived from the people's past state traditions and political organizations, producing accounts that did not always worry too much about such matters as critical methodological approaches to source material or the substantive truth of historical legends: the Golden Age of 'national history' had begun. Past political orders were reinterpreted as the forerunners of the nation-states to come, often in a highly arbitrary fashion. The Greeks had the Byzantine Empire, the Italians the Roman Empire, the Germans the medieval Reich of the Emperors, the Irish the Celtic kingdoms, and the Czechs the ninth-century Slavic kingdom of Moravia. Historians designed pictures of the past which reflected and explicitly served the political aims of the national movement. The existence of historical and mythical states in the dark and distant past was meant to legitimate demands for a nation-state in the present. Memories of heroic eras were constantly being rekindled to bolster national consciousness: the Reconquista and Age of Discovery by the Spanish, the time of the Hussite wars by the Czechs, the history of the early Celtic kingdoms by the Irish, the repulsion of the Turks by the Poles and Hungarians. Likewise, historians claimed that their nation was descended from glorious ancient peoples that had possessed their own state – not only Greeks and Romans, but Celts, Phoenicians, Trojans, Illyrians, Thracians and Teutons too. The boundary between scholarship and national mythology became fluid, particularly in the case of peoples whose existence was practically devoid of known historical roots, for instance Latvians, Estonians and Romanians. Acts such as the founding of the Germanic National Museum in Nuremberg in 1852–53, a 'national institution' whose purpose was to retain and deepen 'knowledge of prehistoric times', and which served as a prototype for similar museums in other countries, testified to the historical and cultural inclinations of Risorgimento nationalism.[7]

Later, monuments were erected in memory of the 'awakeners', rivalling the genuinely national monuments, most of which were designed after the

---

[6] J. G. A. Pocock, 'The Limits and Divisions of British History: In Search of the Unknown Subject', in: *American Historical Review* 87 (1982), p. 321.

[7] Denis Deletant/Harry Hanak (eds), *Historians as Nation Builders. Central and South-East Europe*, London 1988. John Hutchinson, 'Explaining National Revivals', in: *The Australian Journal of Politics and History* 1988. Supplementary Edition, pp. 32–43. Idem, *The Dynamics of Cultural Nationalism. The Gaelic Revival and the Creation of the Irish Nation State*, London 1987. F. A. Wilson, *Folklore and Nationalism in Modern Finland*, London 1976.

national state had been established. These latter frequently celebrated the rebirth of the state and its nationalism with a dramatic sense of pathos, and were intended to deepen national consciousness and popular identification with the new state. Mythological themes were often felt to be the best vehicles for expressing a people's national feeling. In Germany the Arminius monument (Hermannsdenkmal), commemorating the battle of the Teutoburg Forest between Teutons and Romans, was erected in 1875; the Niederwald monument at Rüdesheim on the Rhine was 'consecrated' in the presence of all the German princes in 1883, and the Kyffhäuser monument in Thuringia finished in 1897. Veterans' associations bore a major part of the cost of the latter edifice, as they had done previously for the Niederwald monument with its colossal statue of Germania. Money for the monument to the 'Battle of the Nations' at Leipzig in 1813 which sealed Napoleon's fate, erected between 1898 and 1913, was raised by a specially created League of German Patriots, whose membership rose to thousands. At almost the same time, the enormous marble monument glorifying King Victor Emanuel II and the Italian *risorgimento* was built in Rome. On a more modest scale, the O'Connell Monument in Dublin was unveiled as early as 1882. National monument projects had a lasting impact: at the beginning of the present century, the German architect Theodor Fischer was moved to write that buildings needed to be erected to fashion humanity into a more noble 'common cosmic being'. 'Sacred halls' were needed in which 'man automatically removes his hat and woman restrains her tongue'.[8]

3 The Spread and Organization of Risorgimento Nationalism

In many cases, Risorgimento politicians, whom distorted national historiographies later liked to portray as heroes and champions of freedom, were also poets, linguists or historians. They campaigned in deed and word for their people's cultural maturation and political self-determination in a nation-state. Major obstacles, however, stood between them and their goal: either the nation was entangled politically in one large multinational state; or it was split into a number of particularistic states; or it was divided between several multinational states.

Risorgimento nationalists created political organizations – associations of individuals and groups pursuing shared aims. Hence it can be said that a major feature of modern nationalism since the French Revolution is a concrete mode of social and political organization. The national cause evolves from an intellectual concern of individuals into a broadly based social and hence potentially political force. Except where the process of organization was restricted or, as was frequently the case, prohibited by the existing state, nationalists established cultural and political bodies of varying sizes and degrees of cohesion. If a social group found that the authorities were responding with repression to its attempts to organize

---

[8] Quoted in: George L. Mosse, *The Nationalization of the Masses*, New York 1975, p. 67.

national forces, it tended very often to try and continue illegally. Thus the organizational structure of a nineteenth or early twentieth-century national movement in Europe would depend to a very great extent on the political and legal framework within which it developed.

The two basic strategies open to nationalists – overt or covert agitation – can serve as the starting point for distinguishing between different types of Risorgimento nationalism. Only very rarely do we come across a monolithic, unvariegated national movement that represents the totality of the statements expressing a social group's national goals and the actions with which it pursues those goals. It is much more often the case that at any given juncture a national movement consisted of a mosaic of mutually independent associations and active individuals, each with different ideas about the shape of the future nation-state and the course the national campaign should take. Normally, therefore, any co-operation between them took place on a loose, informal basis. Consequently, it is generally misleading and somewhat inaccurate to speak of *the* nationalism or *the* national movement of Germans, Poles, Italians, Irish or Czechs, for this is to gloss over the not insignificant coloration and variety within the format of the nationalism in question. Moreover, we should remember that organizational structures and modes of propaganda and campaigning change over time. The colourful history of European Risorgimento nationalism provides us with a whole series of examples of this.

With respect to their structural form and method of agitation, the organizations of Risorgimento nationalism can be classified under one of two basic types: constitutional or legalist-reformist; and revolutionary. The former type, for which another name might be evolutionary nationalism, worked to achieve its aims within the legal and constitutional order of a multinational polity, and adopted a pragmatic approach mindful of the feasible and the expedient. It was organized in political parties, clubs, committees, associations, leagues, and student fraternities. The question of whether the national movement regarded itself as a leading élite that, for the time being, dismissed the possibility of extending the organization across the country, or whether it aimed to create a mass movement right from the start, was of paramount importance for the organizational structure of constitutional Risorgimento nationalism. A broad social base obviously needed an appropriately open organizational form: thus Italy saw the creation of the Società Nazionale in 1857, Germany riflemen's, singers' and gymnastics' associations from 1811 onwards and the German National Society in 1859, Ireland had the Irish National League of 1882, while the Bohemian Czechs formed the Sokols, or Falcons, gymnastics societies, in the latter part of the century.

The range of political activities carried out by constitutional associations of Risorgimento nationalism was as broad as their organizational forms. They concentrated on all typical methods of action in the bourgeois public sphere: arranging public meetings and demonstrations, running election campaigns, applying pressure in parliaments, organizing petitions and appeals, leafleting, holding 'national' festivals and reviving celebrations, playing 'national' sports and games, commemorating 'national anniversaries' and nurturing the national language. Revolutionary Risorgimento nationalists, on the other hand, were prepared to break the law and radically change the existing order to achieve their goals. They organized in conspiratorial groups, secret societies and paramilitary associations, advocated the use of force where necessary, and often relied on the support of foreign powers if expedient.

Everywhere, the existing state power responded with all the means at its disposal to the violent methods that were the watchword of the revolutionary brand of Risorgimento nationalism. But European history also provides us with examples of how particularistic states which regarded themselves as the driving force in the process of national unification adopted these very methods. This was true in particular of the establishment of both the Italian and the German national states. Military operations by the Kingdom of Piedmont and Sardinia, as well as popular revolts that were vigorously supported by the Piedmontese government in Turin, forced the annexation of Southern and Central Italy to the Italian national state in 1860. The amalgamation was then given a veneer of legitimation by *ex post facto* plebiscites. A little later, the so-called 'wars of unification' against Denmark in 1864, Austria in 1866 and France in 1870–71 gave birth to the German national state. They were waged largely by that 'German Piedmont', Prussia.[9]

The political praxis of national movements gave rise to overlaps and intermediate varieties between the two major types of Risorgimento nationalism. Members of constitutional bodies frequently had close contact with revolutionary organizations, and on occasion worked in conjunction with them. Constitutional associations could, by choice or dint of circumstance, be transformed into revolutionary groups, and vice versa. In other words, national movements were not static, particularly where they existed over longer periods of time as was the case with Germany, Poland or Ireland. Different elements of the movement rose to prominence at different times. This was due partly to nationalists' own strategic considerations, partly to counter-measures by the authorities that rendered certain forms of organization more expedient than others. There were national movements – in the Scandinavian and Baltic lands, Germany and for a long time in the Habsburg Empire – in which *de facto* the revolutionary, conspiratorial components never played a significant part. In other cases – those in the European part of the Ottoman Empire, or the Polish national movement – revolutionary groups never left the scene.

In other European national movements, revolutionary associations rose to no more than temporary or periodic significance. This happened, for instance, in the case of the Italian Carbonari, a secret organization founded around 1807 in Calabria, which in many ways became the model political secret society of the nineteenth century; and of Giuseppe Mazzini's *Giovine Italia*, a secret society formed in Marseilles in 1831 to pave the way for the revolutionary liberation of Italy.[10] In the ensuing period it was heavily involved in a number of revolts in Italy, and was

[9] William Carr, *The Wars of German Unification*, London 1991.

[10] See Stuart Woolf, *A History of Italy 1700–1860. The Social Constraints of Political Change*, London 1979, pp. 305–16.

the force behind the foundation of Young Europe in Berne in 1834. By contrast, constitutional nationalism dominated in Ireland from the early nineteenth century onwards. There were specific reasons for this. The British parliament was undergoing gradual reform, franchise in the United Kingdom was being widened, and the laws on association, assembly and the press were very liberal by comparison with other countries. All this pushed the vigorous Irish national movement into the realm of open political and parliamentary campaigning. Despite the many oppressive mechanisms operating in Ireland, nationalist faith in the effectiveness of the parliamentary road was strengthened by the fact that at the time the British parliamentary system was constantly proving itself by passing great programmes of reform. The conviction that the national aims of the Irish people could be achieved by presenting them to the British parliament and public in a well-argued and rational manner was, after all, the mainstay in the legitimation of the long-lasting Home Rule movement after 1875. But this approach entailed a long and wearisome process; hence the spasmodic interruptions by revolutionary uprisings and the acts of violence by various nationalist groupings.[11]

4 The Social Structure of Risorgimento Nationalism

The underlying political framework and the intentions of nationalist politicians were not the only factors that had a bearing on the organizational shape of national movements. Their structure was to a considerable degree also a function of the distinctive social strata supporting them, and of the background of their theoreticians and leaders.

Much of the older historical research rigorously maintains that the rising bourgeoisie was almost the sole bearer of European Risorgimento nationalism. As a result 'bourgeois nationalism' is often used interchangeably with the term Risorgimento nationalism. The thesis is accurate to the extent that in almost every case from the French Revolution onwards, small bourgeois élites claiming to speak on behalf of the whole nation formed the heart of the national movements. What is striking, however, is the depth of involvement by the educated middle classes; by comparison, the commercial and industrial bourgeoisie, if it existed, was far less active in national movements. This generally valid observation contradicts the much-cited view of Marx and Engels that the interest of the bourgeoisie in the creation of national states stemmed from its desire to exploit larger markets. The background of the majority of Risorgimento politicians and 'awakeners' of the European peoples was quite different. They were writers, journalists, lawyers, clerics, teachers, low-ranking civil servants, academics, and members of the liberal professions in the widest

---

[11] See D. G. Boyce, *Nationalism in Ireland*, London 1982. Robert Kee, *The Green Flag. A History of Irish Nationalism*, London 1972. *Terrorism in Ireland*, ed. by Yonah Alexander and Alan O'Day, London/New York 1984. Peter Alter, 'Traditions of Violence in the Irish National Movement', in: Wolfgang J. Mommsen/Gerhard Hirschfeld (eds), *Social Protest, Violence and Terror in Nineteenth- and Twentieth-Century Europe*, London 1982, pp. 137–56.

sense of the word. The Frankfurt Paulskirche parliament of 1848–49 has often been described as the 'parliament of professors' on account of its social composition; but in actual fact it was a 'parliament of civil servants'.[12] In this connection, we should also note the phenomenon of the 'intelligentsia', especially in the East-Central European national movements, where the bourgeois classes were still very weak in the nineteenth century.

Thus while it is on the whole correct to see the educated bourgeoisie as the main social bearer and small groups of young intellectuals as the initiators and leaders of Risorgimento nationalism, closer inspection reveals that this formulation is still too vague and undifferentiated. National movements were not simply identical with bourgeois interest or pressure groups. It is equally incorrect to claim, as the historian Piero Gobetti did in the 1920s with reference to the Italian *risorgimento*, that nation-states were the creations of extremely small minorities who managed gradually to win over broad sections of the population to the nationalist cause with the help of modern techniques of mass persuasion.[13] The underlying thesis here of 'intellectual nationalism' or 'élite nationalism' can at best be applied to the early stages in national movements. Literary and intellectual figures were never as deeply involved in the later phases of German nationalism as were, for example, Ernst Moritz Arndt, Friedrich Ludwig Jahn, Johann Gottlieb Fichte, Friedrich Schleiermacher or Theodor Körner during its early phase at the time of the Napoleonic occupation. 'Love of the German fatherland is and must remain first and foremost a cause for the learned, not the commoners,' wrote the Jena professor Jacob Friedrich Fries in 1815.[14]

Once they started campaigning in public, however, the national movements in all countries earned a body of support whose social origin was more variegated than and went far beyond the narrow stratum of the educated middle classes. Nationalism was frequently also embraced by the urban petty bourgeoisie, civil servants, students, the lower rural nobility (particularly in the case of Poles and Magyars), in addition to artisans, peasants and later on even sections of the labour movement. The backing of these classes was crucial for those Risorgimento politicians who conceived the national movement not as pertaining to an élitist clique, but as an organized mass movement whose demands would be substantiated by the sheer weight of public support. In his *Marxism and the National Question*, Stalin looked back on the nineteenth-century national movements with the words: 'The strength of the national movement is determined by the degree to which the wide strata of the nation, the proletariat and peasantry, participate in it'.[15] The lower ranks of the clergy were usually instrumental in incorporating the great mass of the rural population into the movements. In fact religious leaders have played a prominent

---

[12] Lewis Namier, *1848: The Revolution of the Intellectuals*, 6th ed., Oxford 1971.

[13] Piero Gobetti, *Risorgimento senza eroi*, Turin 1926.

[14] Quoted in: Otto Dann, 'Nationalismus und sozialer Wandel in Deutschland 1806–1850', in: *idem* (ed.), *Nationalismus und sozialer Wandel*, Hamburg 1978, p. 113.

[15] Joseph Stalin, 'Marxism and the National Question, in: *idem, Marxism and the National and Colonial Question*, London 1936, p. 15.

part in the history of Greek, Romanian, Slovak, Slovene, Croatian as well as Irish, Baltic and Polish nationalism.

The characteristic differences evident in the social make-up of every national movement depended, in other words, on specific conditions and circumstances; the level of economic development in the region was not the least important among them. As we might expect, the social structure of the German national movement was quite different from those to be found in the Ottoman Empire or Scandinavia. But since the foundations of economic life in many parts of Europe were undergoing radical transformation from the early nineteenth century onwards, the social structure of many national movements also shifted over time; they were by no means constant. At times certain occupational groups were greatly over-represented in the leadership. The nationalism-bearing groups could grow, change, or dwindle. But if we examine the history of European national movements *in toto*, the overall impression is of a continuous process of nationwide integration. Or put another way, national movements almost everywhere expanded by constantly grafting onto themselves new social strata.

In the long term even the organized labour movement could not escape this process, although it stubbornly continued to adhere to the principle of proletarian internationalism. It would thus be erroneous to attribute the national movements to *one* social class, the bourgeoisie; it is much more accurate to describe them as movements transcending class barriers, but usually led by bourgeois strata, in which the political, economic and social interests of the groups involved were not always equally represented. Youth was particularly prominent in the national movements everywhere; in some cases this was apparent in their very names (Young Italy, Young Turks). When Belgium became a state in 1831, young intellectuals could be found in almost every high office.

We can arrive at a rough picture of the way things were by looking at the examples of Germany, Italy and Ireland. During the wars of liberation against Napoleon, German nationalism was mainly embraced by the educated strata, particularly students. But the Rhine crisis of 1840, sparked off by French expansionist ambitions towards that great river, fired nationalist fervour throughout the middle classes – senior civil servants (many of whom had belonged to student fraternities) as well as the commercial and propertied bourgeoisie (particularly in the *Sängerbewegung* – singers' movement), professors as well as artisans. Even the two outstanding monarchs of pre-1848 Germany, Ludwig I of Bavaria and Frederick William IV of Prussia, were sympathetic to the national cause. They shared a penchant for 'romantic German consciousness and a medieval sense of the Empire',[16] and gave their backing to the construction of national monuments. In Bavaria, the Valhalla on the Danube was completed in 1842, and the finishing touches finally put to the Hall of Liberation at Kelheim, near Ratisbona, in 1863, both with the generous help of

---

[16] Theodor Schieder, 'Partikularismus und Nationalbewußtsein im Denken des deutschen Vormärz', in: Werner Conze (ed.), *Staat und Gesellschaft im deutschen Vormärz 1815–1848*, 2nd ed., Stuttgart 1982, p. 22.

the royal purse, while the resumption of work on Cologne cathedral was celebrated in 1842 in the presence of the Prussian king. Singers', riflemen's and gymnasts' associations, along with societies supporting the cathedral project, lent a broad popular base to the national movement. A guard of honour formed by gymnasts who had reorganized in 1842 greeted the National Assembly as it entered the Paulskirche in Frankfurt in 1848. Though the national movement still failed to win solid backing from either the lower classes or the peasants, most of whom were firmly attached to local dynasties and their narrow home environments, the explosive growth in the number of local, regional and 'all-German' associations throughout the cultural nation testified to the fact that from the 1840s onwards it had become a broadly based bourgeois movement. A further indication of the breadth of the national movement during this period was provided by the all-German national festivals, frequent scholars' congresses and the campaigns for the construction of national monuments – 'a release valve for frustrated policies', as the historian Thomas Nipperdey has put it. 'Riflemen and gymnasts hold the Reich steady' ('Die Turner und die Schützen sind des Reiches Stützen') was a popular saying in the early 1860s. An analysis of the social composition of the Leipzig Gymnastics Festival of 1863, in terms of attendance the most important event of this kind in Germany, shows that artisans dominated (60 per cent of all participants), followed by those 'in commerce' (30 per cent), and academics (10 per cent).[17] At this time even the nascent German labour movement counted itself as part of the national movement, adopting a national-democratic stance and the ambiguous slogan 'Freedom through Unity'.

Generalizations about who constituted the Italian national movement also need to be discarded and replaced by more finely tuned conclusions. Recent research has convincingly demonstrated that the creation of the Italian national state cannot be seen simplistically as the work of a rising bourgeoisie conscious of its class identity and interests. Marxist historians of the *risorgimento* in particular have been prone to assume that the Italian bourgeoisie actively pursued the formation of a large national market as an indispensable framework in which to realize its full potential in an age of gradual economic change. This interpretation, however, has been rightly attacked with the argument that, although national unification in Italy was almost contemporaneous with the unification of the German states, the active forces in Italy belonged to classes that, because of different levels of economic development, were far less entrenched than in Central Europe. There must be fundamental doubt about whether an entrepreneurial Italian bourgeoisie with a well defined national programme existed at all in the first half of the nineteenth century. Much suggests that a politically influential middle class did not emerge until

---

[17] Reinhard Wittram, 'Wandlungen des Nationalitätsprinzips', in: *idem, Das Nationale als europäisches Problem. Beiträge zur Geschichte des Nationalitätsprinzips vornehmlich im 19. Jahrhundert*, Göttingen 1954, p. 36. Dieter Dueding, 'The Nineteenth-Century German Nationalist Movement as a Movement of Societies', in: Hagen Schulze (ed.), *Nation-Building in Central Europe*, Leamington Spa 1987, pp. 19–49. Jonathan Sperber, 'Festivals of National Unity in the German Revolution of 1848–1849', in: *Past and Present* 136 (1992), pp. 114–38.

after the national state came into being; the evidence points rather to the existence of fragmented and segmented bourgeois strata in the various pre-unity states. Perhaps only the educational élite and the commercial and industrial middle class in the economically dominant state of Piedmont broadened their horizons beyond their own borders and shared an all-Italian view.

Politically active minorities comprising some of aristocratic descent, others from the educated middle classes more or less thrust their liberal and national manifesto down the throats of Italy's weak and heterogeneous bourgeoisie. As in Germany, the national movement's powerhouse was provided by journalists, writers, academics and lawyers – intellectuals in the broad sense – in conjunction with liberals in the aristocracy and army who were also keen to revise the political order imposed on Italy in 1815. As in Germany too, the supporters of the Italian national movement covered a very wide social spectrum: the influential Carbonaria included members of the academic professions, clerics, well-to-do merchants, businessmen, industrialists, landowners and civil servants. The *Giovine Italia* that Mazzini founded in 1831 recruited from a variety of groups ranging from the nobility through the artisans, to the pre-industrial urban working classes (dockers, building workers, and so on). It was especially popular among lower-ranking officers in the various standing armies. Finally, the *Società Nazionale* of 1857 was dominated by liberal aristocrats and members of the independent professions, though rural landowners, artisans, civil servants, members of the armed forces, the entrepreneurial middle classes in agriculture, trade and industry were also well represented.

Striking differences existed between the social structure of the Italian movement, which from the very beginning was able to extend its appeal above and below the middle classes, and that of Irish nationalism. One of the most fascinating and long-lived instances of its kind among the smaller European peoples, the nineteenth-century Irish national movement, it is frequently said, was one of tenant farmers, peasants and agricultural labourers led by the urban middle classes and the Catholic clergy. Though this is by and large accurate, a more detailed and varied picture emerges if we carefully examine the individual nationalist organizations in Ireland. What we then find is that the early national bodies drew their support almost exclusively from the commercial and educated urban middle classes and the lower ranks of the minority Catholic rural nobility. As time passed, the organizations subscribing to constitutional nationalism were able to make a deeper and more widely felt impact on political life as they won over the rural populace, which was first mobilized for the national cause in the 1820s by the great agitator Daniel O'Connell, aided by the Catholic clergy.[18]

The rural population remained the backbone of constitutional nationalism, right up until the twentieth century; from 1880 onwards, it was represented in the British House of Commons by the Irish Parliamentary

---

[18] Maurice O'Connell (ed.), *Daniel O'Connell. Political Pioneer*, Dublin 1991. James A. Reynolds, *The Catholic Emancipation Crisis in Ireland, 1823–1829*, New Haven 1954.

Party. In the latter part of the nineteenth century, national organizations pursuing different political aims and deriving support from other social groups began to emerge alongside the Parliamentary Party-led Home Rule movement, which by then had swept across most of Ireland. Their origins lay not least in the economic change the country was undergoing. In 1900 the Irish national movement was thus neither a socially nor politically homogeneous force: the 'bourgeois' nationalism of the Home Rulers – the rural population led by the urban middle classes – whose goal was an autonomous Ireland within the United Kingdom, ran parallel with that of the nascent, always small labour movement led by James Connolly, which attempted to marry socialism with nationalism and aspired in the long term to an independent socialist republic. At the same time, a separatist nationalism was flourishing in the shape of associations which, like the labour movement, demanded Ireland's secession from the mainland. They were supported almost exclusively by the growing urban petty bourgeoisie – the class from which Irish nationalism's revolutionary underground also drew its members.[19] The organized labour movement and the revolutionary bodies were together behind the Easter Rising in Dublin in 1916, which paved the way directly for the final stages in the creation of the Irish state. But the Irish national state of 1922 was no socialist republic, but a liberal constitutional state unable to break its ties with the British crown before 1949.[20]

5 Social Change as a Condition of National Movements

For contemporaries, as well as for later historians, the words 'national awakening' of a people essentially meant a process of political mobilization: a process emanating from a minority or social group within a people and gradually embracing ever wider sections of society. As Hans Kohn put it, nationalism demands the 'integration of the masses of the people into a common political form'.[21] This clearly prompts inquiry into what causes the 'awakening' and why the transformation of an unpolitical people into a political nation and its integration into 'a common political form' happened when it did. Yet it is only fairly recently that scholars have started giving proper attention to the conditions under which Risorgimento nationalism – or for that matter, any kind of nationalism – could arise. The important work done by Karl Deutsch on the sociology of communication, particularly his *Nationalism and Social Communication*, first published in 1953, has proved to be a most fruitful stimulus in

---

[19] See Alan O'Day (ed.), *Reactions to Irish Nationalism*, London/Ronceverte (West Virg.) 1987. Sam Clark, 'The Social Composition of the Land League', in: *Irish Historical Studies* 17 (1970–71), pp. 447–69. F. S. L. Lyons, *Ireland since the Famine*, 2nd ed., London 1973. K. Theodore Hoppen, *Elections, Politics, and Society in Ireland, 1832–1885*, Oxford 1984. Tom Garvin, *The Evolution of Irish Nationalist Politics*, Dublin 1981.

[20] Kevin B. Nowlan (ed.), *The Making of 1916. Studies in the History of the Rising*, Dublin 1969. J. J. Lee, *Ireland 1912–1985. Politics and Society*, Cambridge 1989.

[21] Hans Kohn, *The Idea of Nationalism. A Study in its Origins and Background*, New York 1961, p. 4.

this respect. Deutsch attributes the emergence of national consciousness primarily to a more intensive exchange of information, facilitated by a common culture, and to the resultant more concentrated intercommunication within a large social group, or 'community of communication'.

Now, there can be no question that better communication, improved by new modes of transport, innovations in news transmission, higher standards of literacy, the expansion of the press and so forth, provides a crucial environment for the spread of a national consciousness through a given population. But it does not explain why that national consciousness arises. Additional impulses are required before a significant proportion of the population's political energy can be mobilized by national ideology. In this context, the conspicuous connection between nationalism and social change was recognized a long time ago. The striking contemporaneity between national movements and the modernization of social and economic life from the late eighteenth century onwards raised the question of whether modern nationalism, and the Risorgimento variety in particular, could be attributed to certain processes of change within society.[22] The two key secular changes were, first, the dissolution of feudal systems of rule, propelled in France by the impact of the Great Revolution, and, secondly, the industrial revolution, which gradually engulfed every aspect of life. Methods of production changed; customary social relations were shaken as they had never been shaken before; unprecedented numbers of people began living in towns that seemed to explode into existence: the older, familiar world was breaking up. Social disruption, internal migration, pauperism, widening gulfs of social inequality were the side-effects of early industrialization that plunged nineteenth-century European society into a state of continuous instability from which it had not emerged even by the early twentieth century. The right of certain social strata to assume political leadership had been taken for granted; now rising social groups were disputing that right, and it could not be long before they began to insist on participation in government themselves.

Political revolution in France, and industrial revolution emanating from England ushered in an era of accelerated political, economic and social upheaval. If traditional systems of political and social values did not collapse absolutely, they were at least exposed to the pressures of radical change. As industrial society gave rise to division of labour, differentiation of occupations, and specialization, individuals felt that their social environment was no longer a coherent whole. The collapse of traditional legitimacy, of regional and corporate ties, allowed room for new loyalties. In this critical setting of rapid change in almost every sphere of existence, nationalism sketched out a new order for state and society which enveloped individuals who had been left to fend for themselves.

Nationalism provided the individual with a vision of greater scope for personal development and more active involvement in the formation of the nation's political will. The effect was that the struggle against the old feudal regime, against monarchs and dynasties, appeared to be a struggle

---

[22] This was recently rediscovered by Ernest Gellner, *Nations and Nationalism*, Oxford 1983.

for the creation of an egalitarian, democratic and liberal society. Starting from where the French revolutionaries of 1789 had left off, nationalists demanded freedom, equality and self-determination for both nation and individual alike. Modern nationalism espoused desirable political aims; it promised individuals, isolated, though also freed by the break-up of traditional ties, that they would be able to put down new roots in the new community of equals to be constituted. It presented a picture of the world that drew a sharp distinction between friend and foe. Devotion to the nation seemed to become an inner need: the best way to establish personal and supra-individual identity in the post-revolutionary world was to identify with the nation's historical and cultural heritage, with its language, literature and history, its present and future political being. In short, in the transition from the old, agrarian world to the new industrial universe, the ideology of nationalism became an instrument capable of mobilizing and integrating the masses. Yet it could not have evolved into a widely supported movement if the willingness to be mobilized was not already latent within individuals and the masses. Consequently, modern scholarly opinion defines nationalism as both an instrument and off-shoot of social and political mobilization; a motor, and a product of the universal social and political transformation of society to industrialism and the constitutional order.

It takes time for social groups and strata to be politically mobilized. The Czech historian Miroslav Hroch has conducted a comparative analysis of the process and shown that, at least as far as the smaller European peoples in the nineteenth century were concerned, it proceeded in three clearly distinct phases. In the first phase, learned and culturally-minded individuals such as teachers, students, members of the clergy, journalists and writers turned their attention to their people's language, history and culture, though without arousing in society at large any great excitement about things national for the time being; but then, after all, they did not intend to make an impact on the public. Not until the second phase does this learned interest spread to other sectors of the population, when it is transformed into channelled political agitation by a minority that thinks in terms of the nation, whom Hroch calls 'patriots'. Hroch describes this phase (about whose beginning he says nothing precise, however) as the 'fermentation-process of national consciousness', as the real period of 'national awakening'. This decisive stage in the formation of national consciousness is then followed by one in which the national cause is adopted by wide sections of society. As soon as this stage is reached, Hroch says, the people has successfully 'awoken'.[23] Hroch's chronological scheme can be shown to be valid for a number of nations. But he fails to tackle the important problem of transition from one phase to the next; he is silent on the precise impetus that takes nationalist mobilization from one qualitative stage to the next. What we wish to know, however, is just how

---

[23] Miroslav Hroch, *Social Preconditions of National Revival in Europe. A Comparative Analysis of the Social Composition of Patriotic Groups among Smaller European Nations*, Cambridge 1985, pp. 22–23.

and why the interest of a minority élite in the national question becomes the basis of a powerful mass movement.

We have already mentioned the fact that the existence of a developed and rapidly improving network of communication within a large social group is very important for the emergence of a national movement. Certain conditions must obtain before minds are receptive to national slogans and national ideology. Though they occurred at different times and with varying intensities, the factors perhaps most significant in making contact between people easier and setting off the process of nation-building in nineteenth-century Europe, were the expansion of the transport system, the introduction of compulsory schooling, and the unprecedented spread of books, newspapers and journals. Common forms of behaviour, social needs and ideas about political aims and concepts cannot emerge until sections of the population and social strata hitherto isolated from each other are able to communicate. Only then can people become conscious of the commonalities that further social integration, and that can be articulated in politics as nationalism. But this still does not provide a wholly satisfactory answer to why a national movement can gain a broad and vibrant social basis. Apparently some other factor is needed to initiate this.

National movements clearly did receive such impulses. Closer study reveals that in almost every historical instance Risorgimento nationalisms and national movements were occasioned by real or perceived crises. To put it another way: social change, in conjunction with the corrosive impact it had on traditional social and political relations in the many societies undergoing extensive modernization from the late eighteenth century, sufficed to *predispose* individuals and large social groups to integration into a new, national order; but this alone was not enough. It was only by actually living through, or by perceiving there to be a political, economic or social crisis, often by feeling the direct shock of turmoil, that individuals were made receptive to national ideology and willingly embraced national organizations.

As the first seeds of German nationalism, for example, were being sown in the early nineteenth century, the old Holy Roman Empire was disintegrating and Prussian power waning, while Napoleonic rule and French hegemony cast a shadow over the whole country. Later on, the Rhine crisis of 1840 and the conflict with Denmark over Schleswig and Holstein gave a tremendous boost to the national feeling. In a similar fashion, following the failure of the 1848 revolution and the restoration of the Habsburg monarchy in Northern and Central Italy, the Italian national movement gained ground, with Piedmont, economically the most dynamic state, forming the focal point. Czech nationalism 'awoke' in 1848 when the German National Assembly in Frankfurt laid claim to Bohemia as part of the future German nation-state. In Ireland the Home Rule campaign did not acquire the dimension of a mass movement until the serious agrarian crisis struck at the end of the 1870s. Occasionally, *étatisme* – the establishment, for instance, of an 'official language' or a standard education system with prescribed curricula and aims, bureaucratization, centralization and the imposition on life of regulated uniformity – promoted outbreaks of nationalism. A dominant nationalism seeking to assimilate or undermine the power of competing national forces could likewise find that ultimately these efforts were stimulating 'sub-nationalisms'.[24] The histories of the Dual Monarchy, Tsarist Russia and Prussia/Germany provide a whole array of examples of this.

It would be quite correct to say that nationalism in both its liberal and illiberal forms responds to the crisis with a 'kind of counter-utopia of national duties'. These might be founding an ethnically and linguistically homogeneous nation-state, or reclaiming the nation's irredenta.[25] Here too nationalism casts an ambivalent light, for while Risorgimento nationalism strives for political change, its integral counterpart serves to absorb and neutralize the effects of social and political changes. In order to accelerate political development, the exponents of Risorgimento nationalism adopted other, more often than not social goals that were in many cases heavily tinged with millenarianism. The overthrow of the existing political system, they promised, would mean freedom, the end of privilege for the few and a general improvement in everyone's situation. As the Greek struggle for freedom began, Ypsilantis declared in 1821 that victory over Ottoman rule was nigh, and 'with it the advent of all happiness'.[26] Leaders of national movements blamed social and economic troubles on ruling foreign élites, central governments of multinational empires, or a neighbouring country.

As Irish nationalists began to campaign for Home Rule in the 1870s, few people outside the movement grasped all the implications it had for Ireland's domestic order and her constitutional situation within the United Kingdom. But during the agricultural crisis around 1880, Home Rule became the lynchpin of popular hopes and far-reaching expectations. The political mobilization and national integration of the Irish tenants and agricultural labourers was achieved less by the force of rational argument than by the emotional appeal to real individual sentiments and worries. Tenant farmers and agricultural labourers were largely unimpressed by speeches they heard at nationalist meetings on the English system of oppression in Ireland, or the political advantages of Home Rule. 'But when they heard speeches about the land and landlordism and the rights of the people to the soil,' remarks the American historian Norman Palmer, 'their deepest feelings were stirred.'[27] When nationalists' political demands were intertwined with tenant farmers' social and economic grievances, it seemed that the condition of the Irish people would never improve decisively unless Home Rulers had their way. As the nationalist press in Ireland put it at the time, Home Rule was synonymous with a new phase of prosperity in Irish agriculture, an end to landlordism, sweeping changes in people's

---

[24] See above p. 21.

[25] Hans-Ulrich Wehler, 'Zur Funktion und Struktur der nationalen Kampfverbände im Kaiserreich', in: Werner Conze *et al.* (eds), *Modernisierung und nationale Gesellschaft im ausgehenden 18. und im 19. Jahrhundert*, Berlin 1979, p. 118.

[26] See above p. 16.

[27] N. D. Palmer, *The Irish Land League Crisis*, New Haven (Conn.) 1940, p. 115.

living conditions, and a farewell to all the country's long-standing problems. Against a background of latent social conflict and an acute
economic crisis, the Irish national cause was transformed into a mass
movement.[28]

6 Risorgimento Nationalism and its Enemies

That nationalism drew support primarily from the bourgeoisie, who
regarded it as the decisive vehicle for their political emancipation in the
liberal nation-state, is in itself an indication of where we might find its
intellectual and political opponents. The powers of the status quo in the
nineteenth century – primarily the governments of multinational empires
and sovereign princes in small states – used all the means at their disposal
to combat national ideas, movements and aspirations. Dynasties, the
landowning nobility, functionaries, the army, the senior clergy, and not
least the universities had always been ill-disposed towards any form of
revolution, change and modernity. Their prime interest was to defend the
existing social and political system in Europe set out by the Congress of
Vienna in 1815.

The defenders of the status quo regarded national forces as subversive
elements bent on eradicating social difference, dissolving established structures of government, and weakening the monarchical principle. In the
minds of peoples stirring from their sleep, striving for their political and
social liberation, the creation of the nation and nation-state was nothing
if not positive; to the governments and ruling élites of multinational
empires it was nothing but the irresponsible destruction of the tried, tested
and legitimate order of things. In 1849 the Bavarian minister Ludwig von
der Pfordten emphatically warned against the dangers that would be
presented by the kind of division of Europe into nation-states for which
revolutionaries in many parts of Europe had been pressing just one year
earlier. This, he maintained, would be tantamount to letting revolution
in 'through the back door'. Early nineteenth-century Risorgimento nationalism was essentially ranged against Prince Klemens Metternich, the quasi-
omnipotent Austrian Chancellor and Europe's leading statesman in the
period between the Congress of Vienna and the revolutions of 1848.
Metternich saw himself as the creator of the political and social order
of 1815, and as the guarantor of the restored domestic power balances
throughout the continent. No account whatsoever had then been taken of
popular national expectations, let alone of the widespread desire for self-
determination. In the eyes of the Viennese Chancellor, the loosely knit
German Confederation represented the best bulwark against the liberal
and national spirit of the age in Central Europe. He was right to fear the
explosive power of nationalism, for it was precisely in the territories of
the Habsburg monarchy and the surrounding regions of Central, Southern
and South-East Europe that the idea of the self-determining nation and the

---

[28] Conor Cruise O'Brien, *Parnell and his Party, 1880–90*, 2nd ed., Oxford 1964.

sovereign nation-state would go on to celebrate its most glorious triumphs. When this happened, it did so in almost every case at the cost of the multinational imperial states that had evolved over the centuries.[29]

Other political assumptions and convictions based on a range of philosophical foundations, and arousing varying degrees of passion, were a further source of resistance to the nascent nationalism among the European peoples, though such opposition frequently took the form of intellectual disputation against nationalist ideology rather than of an overt political opposition provoking recourse to repressive measures. For the nineteenth-century air also rang with voices arguing that nationalism, the ideology of rising social strata desiring change, did not simply question the validity of the domestic and international status quo, but also posed the most fundamental threat to the peaceful co-existence of peoples. They absolutely rejected the belief, so convincingly elaborated by such as Mazzini in speeches and writings, that nationalism was essentially a force for peace.

Some of the most vigorous opposition to the national principle came from Germans. The very moment the German cultural nation, stirred by the wars of liberation against Napoleon, set out to become a political nation, the great literary master Goethe had nothing but disparaging things to say about the organization of the world into nations and nation-states. His contemporary, Schiller, had anticipated this in 1796, when he wrote in the *Xenien* (Gifts to Departing Guests): 'Germans, you hope in vain to become a nation. Teach yourselves rather to be freer human beings – you can do it.' The poet felt that the culture and character of the German nation had nothing or only very little to do with its political fate. In a similar vein, the Prussian historian and diplomat, Barthold Georg Niebuhr (who is but one example among many), believed that the Germans were, like the ancient Greeks, a cultural community that could easily dispense with the framework provided by a unified national state. Niebuhr must be counted among those who defended the confederalist set-up of Central Europe, and who saw the existing state, not the imagined nation, as the repository of historically legitimated principles of rule. It was a view that asserted the reality of the multitude of German states bequeathed by the Napoleonic era and the Congress of Vienna, and reflected the deep-rooted sense of identity of the individual German states. Nationalists, who were forced to take this current of thought very seriously, derisively described it as 'particularism'. In 1864 for instance, the German historian Heinrich von Treitschke, who also devoted some of his time to journalism, spoke of the 'fairy-tale world of particularism'.[30]

The prominence of the nation-state in the realm of politics and ideas was also a controversial matter in nineteenth-century political literature, even for a broad section of Liberal thought. Some constantly argued that the state should as a matter of principle be deemed superior to the nations. This is somewhat astonishing for an age in which the main current of

---

[29] Alan Sked, *The Decline and Fall of the Habsburg Empire 1815–1918*, London 1989. Oscar Jászi, *The Dissolution of the Habsburg Monarchy*, London 1971.

[30] Heinrich von Treitschke, 'Bundesstaat und Einheitsstaat', in: *idem, Historische und politische Aufsätze vornehmlich zur neuesten deutschen Geschichte*, 3rd ed., Leipzig 1867, vol. 1, p. 448.

politics was running against the old multinational structures. The advocates of particularism in Central Europe were joined in their opposition to nationalism and its goals in particular by those conservatives who favoured a *grossdeutsch* to a *kleindeutsch* Germany. The Innsbruck historian Julius Ficker and the journalist and writer Constantin Frantz were prominent among them in the 1860s and 70s. Their political prototype was the pre-national Holy Roman Empire, whose traditions, they believed, were being legitimately continued by Austria and, in other ways, by the states comprising the German Confederation. The latter had already been described in 1816 as the 'peace-state of Europe'.[31] In the 1870s even Bismarck, who had helped bring about the unification of Germany by violent and revolutionary means, but who had always steered well clear of liberal German nationalism, was moved to defend the multinational state in the interests of his conservative policy of European security. 'The establishment of small national states in Eastern Europe is an impossibility,' he opined in January 1874, since 'only historical states are possible.'[32] In his memoirs he went on to ask: 'Whatever can fill *the* place in Europe that has hitherto been filled by the Austrian state from Tyrol to Bukovina? Any rearrangement in this area could only be of a permanently revolutionary nature.'[33]

The most prominent Liberal champion of the state that housed different nations and nationalities was the Englishman Lord Acton. Having examined the Italian *risorgimento* and Mazzini's ideas, in 1862 he wholeheartedly spoke out against the pure principle of the nation-state that was at the time also being espoused by his compatriot John Stuart Mill. Acton called the 'theory of nationality', by which he meant nationalism, 'a retrograde step in history'. The co-existence of several nations in one state was, rather, the test as well as the best security of that state's internal freedom; it was also 'one of the chief instruments of civilization', which testified to a greater degree of advancement than did national homogeneity. The 'theory of unity makes the nation a source of despotism and revolution'; a state which was incompetent to satisfy the demands of different peoples and nationalities condemned itself, while 'a State which labours to neutralize, to absorb, or to expel them, destroys its own vitality'.[34] These were prophetic words, but they failed to impress Acton's contemporaries. He concluded that 'those states are substantially the most perfect which, like the British and Austrian Empires, include various distinct nationalities without oppressing them.'[35]

Such clarity of judgement was not demonstrated by the leaders of that other great current of the age, socialism. The attitude of the organized labour movement and its theoreticians to nationalism was ambivalent.

---

[31] A. H. L. Heeren, *Der Deutsche Bund in seinem Verhältnis zu dem Europäischen Staatensystem bei Eröffnung des Bundestags dargestellt*, Göttingen 1816, p. 14.

[32] Otto von Bismarck, *Die Gesammelten Werke*, vol. 8/2: *Gespräche*, ed. by Willy Andreas, Berlin 1926, p. 106.

[33] *Idem, Gedanken und Erinnerungen*, Stuttgart 1898, vol. 2, p. 45.

[34] John E. Acton, 'Nationality', in: *idem, Essays on Freedom and Power*, ed. by Gertrude Himmelfarb, London 1956, pp. 159–60, 168.

[35] *Ibid.*, p. 168.

The vast majority of socialists regarded nationalism as an expression of bourgeois society which was no concern of the working class. But although the *Communist Manifesto* of 1848 maintained that working men had no country, they had enthusiastically joined in the national revolutionary battles of 1848–49, particularly in Berlin and Vienna. As far as the Central European labour movement was concerned, it was worth fighting for a democratic national state that guaranteed universal suffrage and tackled the enormous social problems of the day. National unity seemed to be the precondition for solving the social question. Hence the labour movement regarded itself as part of the great movement for national unity and freedom: national-democracy and social-democracy were still closely related. The majority of the 'national' bourgeoisie in 1848–49 had, however, rejected the idea that middle-class nationalism and the national state to which the bourgeoisie aspired should also provide the 'fourth estate' with a framework for emancipation, and hence allow its national integration to proceed on a basis of equality. The decision was to prove a weight around the neck of Central European politics in the years to come. German Social Democrats, for example, who had opposed the German annexation of Alsace-Lorraine in 1870–71, and defended the Paris Commune, were made to feel outsiders in the unified Germany of 1871. The government in Berlin and the bourgeois press spoke of 'enemies of the Reich' and *vaterlandslose Gesellen* ('fellows without a homeland'). However, as the labour movement's trade union and party strength grew it became clear that Social Democrats did not intend to overthrow the newly established German national state by revolution, but at most to transform it from within. The events of August 1914, when the European war broke out, showed that their sense of isolation had finally been overcome by their desire to be part of the nation along with everyone else.

In its clash with nationalism, Central European Social Democracy did not gain much guidance from Karl Marx and Friedrich Engels. Both had referred to the national question with some frequency, but in general they underestimated the political force of nationalism, and failed to undertake a systematic appraisal of the whole problem. In their *Communist Manifesto* of 1848, the two champions of unbending proletarian internationalism assumed that 'national differences and antagonisms between peoples are daily more and more vanishing' owing to the advancement of free trade and to 'uniformity in the mode of production'. Class conflict within the nation would put an end to 'the hostility of one nation to another'.[36] As Herder and Mazzini before them, Marx and Engels believed that the emancipation of peoples would cut away the roots of international tension. Finally, under socialism national boundaries would, like the state, wither away, to be replaced by solidarity across the nations of working people.

Various writers have pointed out that the fathers of the international proletarian movement took a 'dialectical' approach to the issues of nation and nation-state. Their basic thesis led them to believe that the national principle pertained to the bourgeois-capitalist world, and would eventually disappear with it. The national state, they said, represented a transi-

---

[36] Quoted from: *Marx and Engels, Basic Writings on Politics and Philosophy*, ed. by Lewis S. Feuer, 5th ed., Glasgow 1974, pp. 67–68.

tional stage on the way to new forms of society and state.[37] At the same time, they applauded the advent of the Italian and German national states, for they put the labour movement in both countries in a better position: the nation-state could be the vehicle of the proletarian revolution. Marx and Engels greeted Polish and Irish nationalism with exactly the reverse argument. They hoped that Polish and Irish secession would shake the foundations of 'feudal' Tsarist Russia and the capitalist United Kingdom. Nationalism could thus further historical progress in a roundabout way. Such views might well go to explain why the Polish Socialist Party (PPS), a major wing of the Polish labour movement, and the Irish labour movement were both active in their respective national struggles from the 1890s.[38] By contrast, Marx and Engels took a condescending attitude to other nationalities, which they variously described as 'ruins', 'debris' and 'refuse'. We should further note Engels's famous remark about the 'unhistorical' peoples of East-Central and South-Eastern Europe incapable of sustaining themselves.

By the turn of the century, the socialist approach to the national question had cast its net even wider. The Polish-German socialist Rosa Luxemburg, for example, felt that large multinational states like Tsarist Russia should be maintained, and voted against the formation of an independent Polish workers' party, while tactical considerations, particularly with regard to hastening the revolution in Russia, led Lenin to support national movements. Rosa Luxemburg condemned the rising tide of nationalism in the organized labour movement; Lenin pressed for the right of all peoples to self-determination to be incorporated into the Russian Social Democrats' party programme of 1903.

Austrian Social Democrats, whose motivations and aims were different from Lenin's, also tackled the national problem. They produced the most important ideas on the political organization of areas with mixed communities, and on the theory and practice of multinational polities. The great irony is that until 1918, the Austrian Social Democrats belonged with the army and the bureaucracy to the chief mainstays of the Dual Monarchy. Their *Manifesto to the Working People in Austria* of May 1868, produced in German, Czech, Polish, Italian, Romanian and Hungarian, declared that 'the insularity of nationalities is a thing of the past. Today, only a reactionary agenda speaks of the principle of nationalities . . . The labour market does not recognize nationality boundaries, and worldwide communication transcends every language barrier. The omnipresent power of capital, whose expression and standard is money, is indifferent to the presumptions of ethnic origin. Workers of the most varied nationalities labour under the same conditions and are forced to bow to the same economic laws.'[39]

---

[37] Hans-Ulrich Wehler, *Sozialdemokratie und Nationalstaat. Nationalitätenfragen in Deutschland 1840–1914*, 2nd ed., Göttingen 1971, pp. 19 and 212.

[38] Piotr Wandycz, *The Lands of Partitioned Poland, 1795–1918*, Seattle (Wash.) 1974. J. D. Clarkson, *Labour and Nationalism in Ireland*, New York 1925. C. D. Greaves, *The Life and Times of James Connolly*, London 1961.

[39] Quoted in: A. Klíma, 'Die Entstehung der Arbeiterklasse und die Anfänge der Arbeiterbewegung in Böhmen', in: Wolfram Fischer (ed.), *Wirtschafts- und sozialgeschichtliche Probleme der frühen Industrialisierung*, Berlin 1968, pp. 438–39.

Until 1911, Austrian Social Democracy remained a unitary party for the whole of the Dual Monarchy; it was, as Hans Rothfels has said, 'a microcosm of the International'[40] that was at pains to avoid a situation in which conflicts between the nationalities living under Habsburg rule would divide and lame the proletariat. In their attempt to retain Austria-Hungary and turn the empire of many peoples into a supra-national socialist state, a concept was elaborated, mainly by Karl Renner and Otto Bauer, to remove cultural affairs from the aegis of central government, and to guarantee nationalities cultural autonomy. Overall responsibility for economic and social affairs would remain in the hands of the Vienna government. Renner's basic idea was to liberate real economic, social and political interests, which all nationalities shared, from specific national interests. The former could be mediated via the organs of central government, but the democratic machinery of conflict-resolution was, in Renner's view, unsuitable for national questions. The only agencies equipped to decide on individual ethnic allegiance and political loyalty were the individuals themselves. Taken to its logical conclusion, this was a hitherto unprecedented attempt to link together the cultural and political concept of the nation.

The Pan-movements cannot really be said to have been enemies of nationalism unless definitions are qualified; they belonged, rather, to those forces that tried in theoretical and practical ways to overcome nationalism and the division of the world into egotistical nation-states. However, like their modern equivalents, Pan-Africanism and Pan-Arabism, they largely failed to realign nation-states under one wider roof. Either shared geographical or ethno-cultural characteristics were felt to provide the foundations for closer co-operation between nation-states. The earliest movement of this type, Pan-Slavism, which arose in the mid-nineteenth century among the small, western Slav peoples living under Austrian rule, belonged to the latter category. Originally it expressed their desire for closer links with Russia, the only Slav state to which they could turn for protection. The first All-Slav congress was held in Prague in June 1848 just as the German National Assembly in Frankfurt was mooting the integration of Bohemia into the future German national state.[41] But Pan-Slavism soon found its most ardent supporter to be Russia, where it was quickly moulded into a tool of Russian imperialism in the Balkans. The second All-Slav congress convened in Moscow in 1867. The best-known propagandists of Pan-Slavism with a Russian face are the biologist Nikolai Danilevsky, whose *Russia and Europe* of 1869 is often cited as the 'bible of Pan-Slavism', the writer Rastislav Fadeyev, and the journalist Mikhail Katkov. Their dream was a confederation of the Slav peoples under the spiritual and political leadership of the Tsar: the unification of all Slavs 'under Russia's wing', as Fyodor Dostoevsky put it in 1876.[42] This presupposed the dissolution of the Ottoman Empire and the Habsburg monarchy,

---

[40] Hans Rothfels, *Zeitgeschichtliche Betrachtungen*, 2nd ed., Göttingen 1963, p. 100.

[41] See below, p. 77.

[42] M. B. Petrovich, *The Emergence of Russian Pan-Slavism, 1856–70*, New York 1956. Hans Kohn, *Pan-Slavism. Its History and Ideology*, Notre Dame (Ind.) 1953.

as a result of which the Slav peoples of the Balkans frequently invoked Pan-Slavism as a welcome strategic ploy in their struggle for national independence. But the Russian sense of mission was met with scepticism here, too. Pan-Slav notions in the form of 'Yugoslavism' carried most weight when the South Slavs united in 1918 and eventually created Yugoslavia.

Geographical ties and cultural kinship also lay at the root of the other two great Pan-movements in European history. Scandinavianism and the Pan-European movement. Scandinavianism refers to the multitude of aspirations and forces that after Denmark's defeat in the war against Prussia and Austria in 1864 pressed for economic and political unity between Denmark, Norway and Sweden. In the preceding decades, Scandinavianism had been more of a literary and academic movement inspired by Romanticism. Though it failed to catch the imagination, particularly in Norway, which was united with Sweden until 1905, its fruits include the Nordic Interparliamentary Union, which has been in existence since 1907, and the Nordic Council, formed in 1952.

The Pan-Europe Union founded in Vienna in 1923, stemmed from a private initiative by the Austrian Count Richard Coudenhove-Kalergi. It can be seen as a response both to the fractures into nation-states that split Europe after the First World War and to the threat that Bolshevism in Russia was believed to pose for Europe. The aim of the movement, which in fact never managed to build up solid support and suffered rapid decline after 1930, was to unite the European countries into a 'union of common political and economic purpose',[43] the United States of Europe. It is impossible, however, to overlook the impetus that the inter-war Pan-Europeanism gave to the post-1945 politics of European unity.

---

[43] Richard N. Coudenhove-Kalergi, *Pan-Europe*, New York 1926.

4

The Nation-State as a Form of Political Organization

1 The Plurality of States and the Nation-State Principle

As an ideology and organized political movement, nationalism locates the identity of the nation and the state in the nation-state. There should be perfect congruence between political and ethno-cultural unity; the unity of the cultural nation should not be impaired by political borders. In other words, the nation is incomplete without the state, and vice versa. The aim of all national movements, the putative goal of history, the crowning glory of all epochs is the creation of the nation-state. It is the culmination of individual self-determination and of the sovereignty of the people. The yearning for the nation-state has such elemental and innovative force because it is, in the mind of the nationalist, the essence of progress. Of course, the idea of the nation-state did not acquire the capacity to burst the existing state and political order asunder until it was imbibed by a large social group whose linguistic and cultural bonds had a power independent of state structures.

In 1895 the sociologist Max Weber described the nation-state as the 'nation's secular organization of power'. Its creation represents an important, perhaps the decisive stage in the continuous process of nation-building. It is an event steeped in political fervour and the individual's absolute devotion to the cause. Giuseppe Garibaldi, a former Piedmontese navy officer, leading the 'Expedition of the Thousand' to Sicily in May 1860; the battle of Sedan in the Franco-German war of 1870; the Easter Rising in Dublin in 1916; political upheaval in Prague in October 1918: these, and similarly dramatic, even revolutionary scenes, dominate the birth of nation-states. The birth has its midwives; it has its heroes and martyrs; it suffers setbacks, and at times the actors wallow in pathos: all material for rampantly mythologizing and glorifying the national past later on.

The demand for national self-determination has, however, failed to become an established part of international law; it has remained a political principle. Nor is the term 'nation-state' usually used in modern constitutional theory to describe a type of state. It refers more to a particular relation between a state and its people. This people is not merely the aggregate of the populace, but a political community that perceives itself as a nation. The nation, defined in terms of political will, language or culture, lays claim to its own state in which it may realize its full potential, and prosper freely without interference or domination by foreign rule.

Since the French Revolution of 1789, the nation-state has become the sole legitimating principle of the order of states. This is not only true within the theories espoused by European national movements, but beyond them too. As Mazzini elaborated, it is the guiding principle in the construction of a natural world order based on nations. If it is violated, and the cultural nation and the state are not allowed to be identical, people can only feel resentment; a culturally and linguistically homogeneous people loses its liberty and its identity if it is divided between different states. The French Emperor Napoleon III was the first European leader in the nineteenth century to profess support for the nation-state principle. In his view, the settlement of 1815, deemed to oppose the wishes of the peoples, including France, could best be terminated by reorganizing the continent of Europe on a new, national basis. As has been correctly pointed out, the idea of the nation and the principle of the nation-state should be regarded, after all, as 'the decisive phenomenon straddling the ages, the very root of all changes in the relation between states and peoples since the middle of the nineteenth century'.[1]

Risorgimento nationalism does not hold the nation-state to be an end in itself, for the rights of the nation derive from the rights of men that are by definition individual and universal. The liberal-democratic national movements of the early nineteenth century hoped above all that the bourgeois concepts of freedom, democracy and parliamentary government would become reality in the nation-state. They saw the nation-state as being synonymous with a constitutional democratic order. Mazzini spoke of rebuilding Italy as a sovereign nation of free and equal beings. The motto heading the statutes of Young Italy in 1831 ran 'Freedom, Equality, Humanity, Independence, Unity'; and as the German Liberal Philipp Jakob Siebenpfeiffer once summed up, 'The division of Germany is an obstacle on the path to liberty'. Those in the liberal camp who later launched the slogan 'Through Unity to Freedom' saw things in a similar vein. Overall German unity would bring democratic freedoms. The nation, the political community of citizens enjoying equal rights, would take the place of pre-revolutionary feudal society.

The nation-state, moreover, was desirable not only from a political, but also an economic point of view. The economist Friedrich List recognized that the particularism of the German states was applying a brake to economic development in early nineteenth-century Central Europe. He advocated the nation-state as the only way of raising productivity, boosting industrialization and lifting large sections of the population out of the miserable conditions they had to suffer. If Germans wanted to catch up with economically more advanced England, they had only one option – to create the German national state.

---

[1] Lothar Gall, *Europa auf dem Weg in die Moderne 1850–1890*, Munich 1984, p. 21.

During the course of the nineteenth century, the principle of the nation-state established itself with remarkable speed and dynamism as one of the guiding tenets of politics. Historians, political philosophers and political scientists ascribed to it a validity almost on a par with natural laws. As early as 1791, the great Thomas Paine declared in his *Rights of Man* that the national identity of citizens is best guaranteed by the democratic nation-state. He suggested that each nation was entitled to its own system of representative government. 'Sovereignty, as a matter of right', wrote Paine, 'appertains to the Nation only, and not to any individual; and a Nation has at all times an inherent indefeasible right to abolish any form of Government it finds inconvenient, and establish such as accords with its interest, disposition, and happiness.' At about the same time in Germany, Johann Gottfried Herder, that influential prophet of cultural nationalism, declared: 'The most natural state is, therefore, a state composed of a single people with a single national character . . . Nothing seems . . . more clearly opposed to the aims which all governments should have in view than the expansion of states beyond their natural limits, the indiscriminate mingling of various nations and human types under one sceptre.'[2]

The tone was set. In 1836 the Prussian historian Leopold von Ranke identified in nations 'an inclination to be states'[3] which in the past had inexplicably been submerged. The philosopher Georg Wilhelm Friedrich Hegel went so far as to maintain that peoples could only find their true destiny in nation-states. Until they reached that position, their existence amounted to no more than 'prehistory'.[4] World history 'takes account only of those nations which have formed themselves into states'.[5] From there Johann Caspar Bluntschli, a liberal Swiss scholar of international law who lectured in Heidelberg, concluded a few weeks before the Franco-German war broke out in 1870 that: 'Every nation is called upon, and is thus entitled, to form a state . . . The world should be split into as many states as humanity is divided into nations. Each nation a state; each state a national being.'[6]

While the ideas of the nation and the nation-state became the focus of post-1789 political thought, the old multinational states with their dynastic foundations, those 'prisons of the peoples', were denied the right to any future. They were perceived as anachronisms, sore thumbs sticking out in a modern world that was willing to accept a state only if it could prove itself as the creation of a homogeneous nation and the well-deserved reward of its nationalism. The spokesmen and theoreticians of the national

---

[2] Thomas Paine, *Rights of Man*, ed. by Henry Collins, Harmondsworth 1969, p. 165. J. G. Herder, *Sämtliche Werke*, Leipzig 1887, ed. by Bernhard Suphan, vol. 13, Berlin 1911, p. 384.

[3] Leopold von Ranke, *Sämtliche Werke*, Leipzig 1887, vol. 49/50, p. 326.

[4] G. W. F. Hegel, *Lectures on the Philosophy of World History: Introduction*, transl. by H. B. Nisbet, Cambridge 1975, p. 134.

[5] *Ibid.*, p. 96.

[6] J. C. Bluntschli, 'Die nationale Staatenbildung und der moderne deutsche Staat', in: *idem, Gesammelte kleine Schriften*, vol. 2: *Aufsätze über Politik und Völkerrecht*, Noerdlingen 1881, p. 90.

movements felt nothing but disdain for Europe's old regimes that embodied an age before the nation-state; their thoughts turned to the revolutionary overthrow and replacement of these relics, whose demise would be simply the execution of a long-overdue judgement of history. According to the Italian jurist and later minister Pasquale Mancini in 1851, a state in which 'many mighty nationalities are forced into unity' was not a 'political corpus' but 'a monster bereft of vitality'.[7] Thomas G. Masaryk, the founder of the Czechoslovak state in 1918, regarded the Habsburg Empire as the negation of the modern state and modern nationality.[8] In the years before 1914 this kind of view was almost commonplace.

The emancipatory thrust of Risorgimento nationalism was consequently a dangerous explosive that threatened to blow the great multinational and hence multilingual empires to smithereens, and thereby to rock the entire European order. It was a major contributory factor in the fall of the Habsburg monarchy, the Ottoman Empire and Tsarist Russia. By the 1870s at the very latest, Irish nationalism was recognized as a national problem even in the United Kingdom of Great Britain and Ireland, one which placed a heavy burden on British politics and which was only partially resolved when the Irish Free State parted ways with the mainland in 1921–22.

The predominance of the nation-state principle since the early nineteenth century has led to the situation today in which the international order is basically structured by the plurality of states. Though the principle could not be applied with absolute consistency in every case, it has proved to be the most enduring of the forces of change in the world of states. The process of nation-building and the emergence of nation-states has fundamentally redrawn the political map, first of Europe between the Congress of Vienna and the 1919 Paris Peace Conference, and then of Asia and Africa in the present century, particularly after the Second World War. Both the advent of nationalism and democracy in Europe from the early nineteenth century onwards, and the twentieth-century liberation of peoples from colonial rule in the Third World, wrested by violent or peaceful means, have brought about a steady, at times convulsive rise in the number of nation-states (Table 4.1). In Europe, it peaked at the end of the First World War with the creation of seven new states, and it peaked again in the closing years of the twentieth century. Once the process of decolonization had begun after the Second World War, Africa alone witnessed the birth of more than fifty states – and there are probably several more in the wings.

States have continually emerged: polities with varying sizes of population and territory, of varying political significance and economic power. Between them they present a picture of an increasingly fragmented international arrangement constantly in flux. By contrast, the dynastic principle,

---

[7] Quoted in: Theodor Schieder, 'Idee und Gestalt des übernationalen Staates seit dem 19. Jahrhundert', in: *Historische Zeitschrift* 184 (1957), p. 336.

[8] *Idem, Nationale und übernationale Gestaltungskräfte in der Geschichte des europäischen Ostens*, Krefeld 1954, p. 5.

Table 4.1 The foundation of states in Europe, 1815–1922

1830	Greece
1831	Belgium
1861	Italy
1871	German Reich
1878	Romania, Serbia, Montenegro
1905	Norway
1908	Bulgaria
1913	Albania
1917	Finland
1918	Poland, Czechoslovakia, Estonia, Latvia, Lithuania, Kingdom of the Serbs, Croats and Slovenes (renamed Yugoslavia in 1929)
1922	Ireland

particularly after primogeniture had been established, had unmistakably furthered the agglomeration of disparate and unrelated regions into larger state entities.

Perhaps the simplest and clearest illustration of the impact the nation-state principle has had is given by the number of formally independent states in the world since the nineteenth century. Between 1870 and 1914, there were around fifty sovereign states in all, sixteen of them in Europe. The figure barely fluctuated over the period. By the end of the First World War the community of states had grown by ten as new states emerged in Europe and the white dominions of Australia, New Zealand and the Union of South Africa gained full independence. When it was founded in 1920 the Geneva League of Nations had 42 members; its successor, the United Nations, was set up in 1945 with 51, but membership had increased to 82 by 1960, 135 by 1973, and 184 by early 1994. For a variety of reasons some states have not joined the United Nations, and new states are still emerging as decolonization and the break-up of multinational states proceeds. Hence it is occasionally suggested that the world will comprise some two hundred states by the end of the century, the majority of them 'mini-states' such as St Kitts and Nevis in the Caribbean, an island of 260 km² and 40,000 inhabitants that gained independence in 1983, or the Pacific island state of Nauru of 21.3 km² and a population of about 9,500. There would seem to be no ceiling on the potential number of independent political entities. Guidelines to the size of territory and population of a nation-state do not exist, nor is there a convincing case for refuting a people's desire for independence in their own state.

2 Stages in the Formation of European Nation-States

In Europe, the nation-state principle established itself in three fairly distinct chronological phases, each of which had its own geographical location too. Theodor Schieder's works on nationalism and the nation-state have been most important in the elaboration of this tripartite pattern. According to him, the first phase was characterized by the emergence of the west European, integrating type of nation-states based on shared political history and the revolutionary transformation of princely absolutism. The state of the old regime became the organ of a self-governing society of responsible citizens held together by the concept of the political nation. Relevant examples of this type of nation-state since the sixteenth and seventeenth centuries are England, the Netherlands, France, and to a certain extent Sweden.[9]

The second phase in the formation of nation-states was dominated by the concept of the cultural nation, and the geographical focus had now shifted to Central and Southern Europe. Here small particularistic states, often with long historical pedigrees, were unified into overarching nation-states in the nineteenth century. Italy and the German Reich are classic examples of divided parts of a nation being rolled into one. Nationalist forces combined with the power interests of a single dynamic state – Piedmont in Italy, and Prussia in Germany. After national unification, the old smaller states were either dissolved and replaced by a centralized administrative apparatus (as happened in Italy), or relegated to a lower degree of sovereignty (as was the case in the German Reich). Almost inevitably the internal structure of these two new national states was heavily influenced by the single power providing the motor of development. Thus the Germany of 1871 was a federation, but its federal elements formed a substratum below Prussian hegemony. The Prussian dynasty in the form of a rejuvenated German 'Kaisertum' rose, as did its Piedmontese counterpart in Italy, to the head of the national state and the Prussian capital Berlin became the capital of the German Reich. Later on the Serbian monarchy also tried to assert a hegemonial grip over the south Slav peoples, but was far less successful than the Piedmontese and the Prussians.

The third phase in the emergence of the European nation-states, likewise dominated by the concept of the cultural nation, relates to the foundation of states in the east-central and south-east regions of the continent in the nineteenth and early twentieth centuries. The key development here was the secession of national entities from large multinational empires. The Ottoman Empire in the Balkans was gradually disintegrating under the weight of constant battles with Christian forces, while the Russian empire of the Tsars and the Habsburg monarchy were collapsing, or were at least being severely weakened, under the impact of revolution and the First World War. The peoples living in these regions regarded themselves primarily as linguistic and ethnic communities. Their political consciousness was not developed *within* and *via* the state; it derived from their opposition to the existing order, which was perceived as alien and destructive of their own national traditions.

The entire band of states stretching from Finland in the north, via the Baltic states to Poland and Czechoslovakia, and on to Albania, Romania and Greece in the south are the products of political secession. Some west

---

[9] See, in particular, *idem, Der Nationalstaat in Europa als historisches Phänomen*, Cologne 1964, pp. 15–17. For the English case: Alan Smith, *The Emergence of a Nation State. The Commonwealth of England 1529–1660*, London 1984.

European nation-states also came into being by breaking away from larger dynastic entities. Thus Belgium left the United Netherlands in 1831; an independent Norway emerged after dissolving its union of 1814 with Sweden; southern Ireland divorced itself from Britain; and finally Iceland ended its union with Denmark in 1944. The examples of Poland's reunification in 1918 of the three areas into which it had been partitioned, and in a different manner the south Slavs highlight the fact that secessionist movements are often simultaneously movements for unification. In these instances we are forced to modify somewhat the three-phase geographical and chronological model of nation-state formation.

By grouping together the European nation-states according to a genetic scheme of ideal types that simplify highly complicated processes, we gain fresh insight into the ability of nationalism, already mentioned above, to adapt and change. We see that as a dynamic political force in the destruction and construction of state entities nationalism is restricted neither to a particular form of society, nor to a particular order of state. It is much more the case that nationalism and its product, the nation-state, varies according to the conditions of the age. Modern nation-based Europe has generated nation-states of differing quality and form; since the early nineteenth century there have been monarchical, republican and dictatorial forms of nation-states, and a range of societal structures exhibiting varying degrees of democracy and authoritarianism. Nationalism is a chameleon-like phenomenon of modern society, but one whose ancestral roots undeniably lie in the French Revolution. This is reflected not least in the form and ideology in which the actual creation of the state is embedded: the convocation of a national assembly; the drawing up of a national constitution based, apart from minor alterations, on the French prototype; the choosing of national symbols such as a flag, anthem and national holiday. It is obvious until today that the symbolic foundation of the nation-state follows a general pattern laid down very early in the history of modern nationalism.

In the Balkans various factors already at work in the early nineteenth century helped nation-states to crystallize: growing internal and external strains on the Ottoman Empire; the keen interest of the great powers in how the fate of the 'sick man of the Bosphorus' would affect the European balance; the fear of the continent's statesmen about a strengthening of Russian and Habsburg influence in the Near East. The formation of nation-states in the Balkans was a stepwise process accompanied by serious political crises.[10] The general pattern was, first, for the Balkan peoples to gain the status of autonomy, while the Sultan retained sovereignty over them. Most were unable to throw off Ottoman rule entirely until much later, and only when Europe's great powers intervened. In the course of this process the territories of these and other new nation-states underwent changes, often for decades, especially in East-Central and South-Eastern Europe. On the whole few European nation-states still have the same borders in which they were first constituted: Belgium, created in 1831,

---

[10] Charles and Barbara Jelavich, *The Establishment of the Balkan National States, 1804–1920*, London, Seattle 1977.

and Norway, created in 1905, are examples. There were a number of reasons for this. A major consideration was of course the interest of the great powers in territorial arrangements. Europe's leaders were clearly concerned enough about political equilibrium to avoid sudden changes and upheavals. In the aftermath of revolts against Ottoman rule, Serbia, for instance, was not given independence but the status of tributary principality of the Sublime Porte in 1815. Following further disturbances in 1830 it became an autonomous principality, still nominally under Ottoman suzerainty. Serbia had to wait until the Congress of Berlin in 1878 before being recognized as an independent state. Four years later it became a kingdom that perceived itself as the core of a future South Slav state, and had particular designs on Habsburg territory. In 1913 the Treaty of Bucharest gave Serbia northern Macedonia; after the First World War it became the centrepiece of the Kingdom of the Serbs, Croats and Slovenes, renamed Yugoslavia in 1929.[11]

The sovereignty of independent Greece was guaranteed by Britain, France and Russia in 1830. From the very outset, its inhabitants regarded their state as the germ cell of a much larger political entity that would embrace their compatriots living in distinctly Greek communities beyond its then existing borders. The question, however, of what would happen to these minorities, which were spread throughout the Ottoman Empire, was never fully answered. The Greek state as constituted in 1830 covered no more than 48,000 km^2, mainly comprising the Peloponnese, the islands of the western Aegean, Attica and Phocis, but it expanded in the ensuing period. In 1863 Greece gained the Ionian Islands, which had been under British protection since 1812; in 1881 almost the whole of Thessaly and a corner of Epirus were added. In the Balkan wars of 1912–13 against Turkey, the Greek national state won southern Macedonia, southern Epirus and the islands of the eastern Aegean from Thasos to Samos, plus Crete, whose populace had risen against Ottoman rule on several occasions in the nineteenth century. The 'great idea' of Greek nationalism – the 'Megali Idea', the hope for the resurrection of the Byzantine Empire – was directed towards Thrace, Constantinople and the coastlands of Asia Minor. But the Treaty of Sèvres (10 August 1921) between the Allied Powers and Turkey only yielded Thrace.[12] The islands of the Dodecanese, occupied by Italy after the Italian–Turkish war of 1911–12, did not become Greek until 1947, when Greece's territory rose to 132,000 km^2. By this time there was only one area inhabited mainly by Greeks which still lay outside the national state: Cyprus, an island with the status of British Crown Colony. The Greek majority (80 per cent of the Cypriot population) aspired to *enosis* – unification with Greece – but their hopes were dashed after a long struggle. The island was never incorporated into the Greek state out of consideration for the Turkish minority, who could count on support from Ankara. Cyprus gained independence in 1960.

---

[11] Marian Kent (ed.), *The Great Powers and the End of the Ottoman Empire*, London 1984. Dimitrije Djordjevic (ed.), *The Creation of Yugoslavia 1914–1918*, Santa Barbara (Calif.) 1980.
[12] Douglas Dakin, *The Unification of Greece 1770–1923*, London 1972.

Italy provides another example of the flexibility of a national state's territory, for it took more than sixty years to settle into its final shape. The Kingdom of Piedmont and Sardinia, under the leadership of its dynamic prime minister Cavour, a major architect of the *risorgimento* until his sudden death, was economically and politically the most powerful Italian state and acted as the driving force behind unification. With French help and despite intense Austrian resistance, the Kingdom of Italy constituted in 1861 comprised the whole of Southern and Central Italy bar the Papal States. As a result, Florence acted as capital city between 1865 and 1871. In the north, Piedmont and Lombardy counted as parts of the Italian national state. Venetia did not join until 1866, a fruit of Italy's alliance with Prussia against Austria in the war of the same year. Finally in September 1870 Italian troops occupied Rome when the French, who had protected the Papal seat from Italian intervention since 1860, lost to Germany and evacuated the city. But even after the prize of Rome, Italian nationalists maintained that Italy was not fully grown, for the populations of Trieste and the Trentino, most of whom spoke Italian, still lived under Austrian rule. The problem of *Italia irredenta*, unredeemed Italy, was solved by the First World War to the extent that the Italy of 1919 had reached its allegedly natural frontiers by gaining the Brenner Pass in the Alps. But at the very moment when nationalist Italians felt that they had at long last satisfied the nation-state principle, at least as far as they were concerned, it was seriously violated. German-speaking South Tyroleans, and the almost half-a-million Croats and Slovenes in Istria and in the area around Trieste, which had been promised by the Allies to Italy as a spoil for its war effort, created new and severe ethnic minority problems.[13] The state's national cohesion had already been seriously called into question by the tensions between economically developed Northern Italy and the backward regions of the Mezzogiorno. The nation-state principle, for that matter, hardly justified Italy's territorial gains after the First World War.

3 The Boundaries of the German Nation-State

For a long time Germans, too, were unable to settle a heated controversy over the shape their nation-state should finally take, and German nationalism became increasingly invigorated by the issue from the 1830s onwards. The vast majority of those in the national movement initially took it for granted that 'Germany' also included the German-speaking territories of Austria. But when the course of the German border was being fixed, decisions were taken, especially between 1864 and 1871, that on the one hand left sections of the German cultural nation outside the newly formed national state, and on the other forced foreign nationals, such as Danes, Poles, Alsatians, Lorraines, Walloons, to live inside the boundaries of the German Reich, in most cases against their will.

---

[13] Anthony E. Alcock, *The History of the South Tyrol Question*, London 1970.

It had become clear as early as 1848–49, when the Revolution signalled the first serious attempt to establish a German national state against the interests of the many particularist principalities, that the question of boundaries would present problems. Although the German national movement celebrated the March Revolution as if it had finally vanquished the dominant dynastic powers in the German Confederation, it lacked a well defined national programme only waiting to be implemented. It could not have one because the movement suffered from too many internal splits. Despite this, in the first half of 1848 the Frankfurt National Assembly was almost unanimous in the belief that the new German Reich should cover exactly the area constituting the existing German Confederation. The concept of the political nation was invoked to underpin this ambition: it was often said in Frankfurt that anyone who lived on German soil was a German. At this stage, however, no solution was yet proffered to the question of what would happen to ethnic Germans residing outside the Confederation's borders, particularly those in Schleswig, East Prussia and the Posen province.

In the autumn of 1848 the parliamentarians in Frankfurt began to tackle a problem that had likewise been left to one side: how would German-speaking Austrians be brought into the new Reich? Should the historic state of the Habsburgs, including the parts of it that lay outside the German Confederation, belong to the German national state? The answer to the latter question was soon a decisive 'no'. The Frankfurt Parliament rightly felt that the national character of the future German Reich would be lost if the whole of the Habsburg monarchy with all its nationalities were drawn in. Understandably the Viennese government voiced its opposition to the idea that Austria could be politically divided. As a result, a compromise plan envisaging a dual confederation of Germany and Austria was discussed in the autumn of 1848, according to which the German Reich would forego those parts of the existing German Confederation that lay inside the Austrian Empire. With the exception of Austria, all German states would instead form a federation, the Reich, which, with the Habsburg monarchy, would slot into another federation governed by the principles of international law. Here were the first contours of the *Kleindeutschland* – 'lesser' Germany, that is: a state without the German-speaking areas of Austria – that was to emerge in 1871. As Prussia went from strength to strength and became the leading force in the unification process after the 1850s, the 'lesser' German option progressively shifted to the fore.

Gradually, a looser conception of the dual confederation evolved, and the original idea of a unitary, complementary whole lost currency; as it did so, the Frankfurt parliamentarians became more sympathetic towards the *kleindeutsch* solution. But they were not yet entirely convinced. After a debate on Austria in the autumn of 1848, however, there was a majority in favour of a German national state consisting of the territory of the former Confederation plus Schleswig, West and East Prussia and a large part of the province of Posen, though fine differences of opinion remained and some delegates still had their reservations. The parliament realized that this answer to the intricate question would mean including national minorities in the new Germany. Their legitimate rights, including that to the unhindered 'development of their ethnic cultural life,' had already been recognized in the generous declaration on the protection of nationalities made by the Frankfurt Assembly on 31 May 1848. The essence of the declaration made its way into Article 188 of the Reich Constitution of March 1849.[14]

The main tenor of the debates in the Frankfurt Assembly over Schleswig was that in terms of language the territory belonged to Germany, even though it was also the home of a large Danish-speaking minority. History, moreover, strengthened the rectitude of Germany's claims: Holstein's membership of the German Confederation was stressed, and the indivisibility of the two duchies of Schleswig and Holstein championed as a matter of historical principle. Given this attitude, the British historian Lewis Namier has criticized the nationalism of the Assembly as illiberal and related it directly to later, more aggressive forms of German nationalism. He referred, in particular, to the approach of the German National Assembly to Posen to back up his argument.[15] More recent research in the way national questions were dealt with in Frankfurt fail, however, to corroborate the kind of simplistic view offered by Namier.[16]

Just as Danish nationalists had objected to the proposed course of the German border in the north, Polish and German nationalism clashed over Posen. Risorgimento nationalists had not envisaged such conflict; as disciples of Herder and Mazzini they proceeded from the assumption that the collapse of the pre-national order in Central Europe would herald the 'springtime of nations' and a policy of reconciliation among free nations. The Revolution's early successes engendered an optimistic belief that the representatives of the liberated peoples would have no difficulty in resolving national conflicts in a spirit of fraternal give-and-take once the old selfish dynasties had been removed from the stage. Nationalism would create a peaceful world.

Yet spring passed quickly. By the end of the revolutionary year 1848 old wounds in German–Polish relations were re-opened and festered for decades, adding considerably to the poisonous myth that the two peoples were hereditary enemies. In the Grand Duchy of Posen after 1815, Prussia had heeded the decisions of the Congress of Vienna and allowed the Polish population their own national organizations; now events overtured the decline of the German goodwill towards the Poles that had characterized the 1830s, and a new round of tensions.

From 1848 onwards, the Prussian government in Berlin worked to incorporate the province of Posen into the German Confederation and the future national state. While its integration policy met with little resistance in East and West Prussia, interests could not have been more sharply

---

[14] See Harm-Hinrich Brandt, 'The Revolution of 1848 and the Problem of Central European Nationalities', in: Hagen Schulze (ed.), *Nation-Building in Central Europe*, Leamington Spa 1987, pp. 107–34. Franz Eyck, *The Frankfurt Parliament, 1848–1849*, London/New York 1968.

[15] Lewis Namier, *1848: The Revolution of the Intellectuals*, 6th ed., Oxford 1971, p. 33.

[16] See, for example, Guenter Wollstein, *Das 'Großdeutschland' der Paulskirche. Nationale Ziele in der bürgerlichen Revolution 1848/49*, Düsseldorf 1977.

opposed in Posen, which in 1846 was inhabited by 1.4 million people. Two-thirds of them were Poles who felt they were the inheritors of a Polish national state yet to be created, and rejected absolutely the idea of living in a German nation-state. In July 1848, following a heated debate in which the opposing national conceptions were mooted, the National Assembly in Frankfurt voted to divide the Grand Duchy between the two peoples. This provoked objections from those Poles, however, who hoped to restore Poland's historical frontiers. But their entreaties fell on deaf ears in Frankfurt.

As the unforeseen, revolutionary consequences of the nation-state principle for the dynastic structure of the Prussian state became ever clearer, the Berlin government set sail on an anti-Polish tack involving the suppression of any Polish national aspirations whatsoever. Most delegates in the Assembly in Frankfurt wanted Germany to have the upper hand over Polish nationalism and did not voice dissent. In essence they were tacitly condoning Prussia's course and ignoring Polish desires for independence.[17] At the international level, Prussia's anti-Polish policy created a stable interest alliance with Tsarist Russia, which was having similar problems with its Poles, that lasted until the eve of the First World War.

A further outcome of the tumultuous events of 1848–49 was that the German national state would not include one of the heartlands of the old Holy Roman Empire, Bohemia, whose inhabitants mainly spoke Czech. The Slav population in both Bohemia and Moravia had adamantly refused to elect delegates to the German National Assembly. In declining his invitation to Frankfurt, one of the leading spokesmen of the Czech-speaking Bohemians, the Prague historian František Palacký, also expressed his commitment to the multinational Habsburg state – ' . . . a state, the maintenance, integrity and strengthening of which is, and must remain, a noble and important duty not only for my people, but for the whole of Europe, indeed for humanity and the civilized world'.[18] Palacký did not believe there was a place for the Czech nation in a German national state, though there was one in the land of the Austrian Emperor. In Bohemia too, where historic territory did not correlate with linguistic and ethnic nationality, the 'springtime of nations' ultimately caused national conflicts to surface. Tensions failed to dissipate even after the Habsburg Empire split up, and persisted right up to the Second World War. The more than 300 participants at the first All-Slav congress that met in Prague in June 1848 rebuffed once again the German National Assembly and its 'greater' Germany. They elaborated a conception of a state that presaged the Czechoslovakia that was to emerge in 1918.[19]

The attitude of Bohemian and Moravian Slavs in revolutionary 1848 strengthened sympathy in the German national movement for the 'lesser' German solution that would, at least for the time being, exclude those Germans living in the multinational state of the Habsburgs. In April 1849

---

[17] Michael Hughes, *Nationalism and Society. Germany 1800–1945*, London 1988, pp. 91–100.
[18] František Palacký, *Gedenkblätter. Auswahl von Denkschriften, Aufsätzen und Briefen*, Prague 1874, pp. 149–51.
[19] Lawrence D. Orton, *The Prague Slav Congress of 1848*, New York 1978.

the Prussian king Frederick William IV had rejected out of hand the suggestion of the Frankfurt Assembly that he be crowned emperor of a 'lesser' Germany; but this did not prevent Prussia now adopting as its own the national concept of the delegates in Frankfurt, and trying initially to put it into practice via a League of German Princes. Though Austria managed to foil Berlin's aspirations once again (in the Punctation of Olmütz in 1850), the course of Central European politics seemed to have already been set.

As a result of these developments, it was often said that the German Reich of 1871 – the work of the Prussian prime minister Otto von Bismarck – was an 'unfinished' national state, since it did not include all Germans, especially German-speaking Austrians. Even advocates of the 'lesser' Germany agreed. After the collapse of the venerable Habsburg monarchy in 1918 the victorious allied powers still prevented a 'greater' Germany being established by leaving in the hands of the new Czechoslovak state those marginal regions of Bohemia inhabited by Germans (Sudetenland), and by outlawing German annexation of Austria. In the years after the war the Austrian republic, whose constitution of 1918 defined German-Austria as a 'constituent part of the German Republic', regarded itself as a 'state against its own will'.[20] The historian Andreas Hillgruber has in retrospect stated that the best Germans could hope for in the nineteenth century and after was 'to gain a national state that was unfinished and that never could be finished; even this could only happen under extremely propitious international circumstances'.[21] As a product of the violent politics of National Socialism, the 'Greater Germany' of 1938 (*Großdeutschland*) which incorporated all Germans living in distinguishable communities, was but a short interlude.

The 'lesser' German Reich of 1871, which suffered territorial losses after defeat in 1918, was also home to other national minorities: Danes in the north, Poles and Masurians in the east, Alsatians and Lorraines in the south-west, Walloons in the area around Eupen and Malmédy – some four million people in all, or six per cent of the Reich population. The architects of the Treaty of Versailles tried, with some success, to redress the balance. Alsace-Lorraine was returned to French rule, for example. On the other hand, the Treaty created entirely new problems of national minorities, particularly in East-Central Europe where a combination of German irredentism and the irredentism and revisionism of other nations placed an enormous strain on international relations between the wars. After 1918–19 the term 'national minority' became an accepted part of political language, and a recurrent theme of international negotiations.

---

[20] Helmuth Rumpler, 'Österreich. Vom "Staat wider Willen" zur österreichischen Nation (1919–1955)', in: Josef Becker/Andreas Hillgruber (eds), *Die deutsche Frage im 19. und 20. Jahrhundert*, Munich 1983, pp. 239–67.
[21] Andreas Hillgruber, 'Die Deutsche Frage im 19. und 20. Jahrhundert – Zur Einführung in die nationale und international Problematik', in: Becker/Hillgruber (eds), p. 15.

4 Nation-States and Multinational States

After new states had risen like a wave sweeping across the land between Finland and Yugoslavia, it seemed in 1918 as though the nation-state principle, held up by many contemporaries and historians as the hallmark of European history after the mid-nineteenth century, had finally become reality. But this triumph was an illusion, a cliché which contemporary observers and historians since then often employed to interpret the world around them. From a modern perspective it is more accurate to say that Europeans were living in an age of sovereign states, the vast majority of which derived their legitimacy from the nation-state principle and the right of self-determination.

Although the nation-state principle appeared to have triumphed, national states with a homogeneous population were still a rarity after 1918, particularly in East-Central Europe and the Balkans where the homelands of nations and nationalities overlap until today. Here it proved fundamentally impossible to create 'pure' or 'genuine' nation-states that were just and acceptable to everyone. In the inter-war period Poland, Czechoslovakia and Yugoslavia were prime examples of 'false' nation-states. Between 1918 and 1920 Polish frontiers were determined by agreement, plebiscite and war (against Soviet Russia in 1920), with the result that according to official Polish figures, 14 per cent of the population were Ukrainian, 3 per cent Byelorussian, 10 per cent Jewish, 2.3 per cent German and 3 per cent of other nationality. Owing to the unbridled nationalism of the new nations invested with the power of state, and the existence of minorities who were often treated as second-class citizens, the nation-state principle failed the test as a means to establish stable political structures in this part of Europe. The political nation proved to be an unworkable concept, while the idea of the linguistically and culturally oriented nation reigned almost supreme.

In the ensuing period, none of the new states in East-Central Europe and the Balkans was able satisfactorily to solve the problems presented by national minorities, by giving generous guarantees of cultural autonomy, for example, or by allowing sound federalist structures to develop. Agreements on the protection of minorities, signed at the Paris peace negotiations in 1919 in recognition of the intermingling of nations in the region, largely failed because they only covered some of the states in which such situations obtained. Formal guarantees of equal rights for all citizens could not be enforced in practice, and in most cases national minorities were subject to the whims of the dominant majority.[22] After 1925 Switzerland had hosted the European Congress of Nationalities, a forum created by as many as twenty-one European minority groups. Although it managed to develop pioneering ideas for pragmatic policies on minorities and nationalities, it made little impact on the outside world. No less important a statesman (and historian) than Winston Churchill wrote in

---

[22] Alan Sharp, 'Britain and the Protection of Minorities at the Paris Peace Conference, 1919', in: A. C. Hepburn (ed.), *Minorities in History*, London 1978, pp. 170–88. I. L. Claude, *National Minorities*, Cambridge (Mass.) 1955.

retrospect a few years after the Second World War: 'There is not one of the peoples or provinces that constituted the Empire of the Habsburgs to whom gaining their independence has not brought the tortures which ancient poets and theologians had reserved for the damned.'[23]

The obvious question – would not the multinational empires of Europe, though anachronistic from a nationalist point of view, ultimately have provided a more suitable political structure – was seldom posed at the time, let alone properly answered. The leaders of national movements were too deeply immersed in irredentism and the complicated national hotch-potch of East-Central Europe and the Balkans to stand back and reflect upon the problematic of the nation-state; the issue was repressed and evaded. There is evidence, however, that the arbiters of nationalist feeling were occasionally overcome by a sense of gloom as they realized that the national homogeneity to which they so fervently aspired could ultimately only be brought about via enforced assimilation, resettlement, expulsions, and even the 'liquidation' of national minorities.

The treatment national minorities have endured in the twentieth century can thus be regarded as a special case of political persecution, founded upon the prejudice that they would be hostile to the ruling power and maintain close ties to related groups abroad in the manner of a 'fifth column'. This prejudice encouraged sections of the majority groups to advocate assimilation and hence exerted even greater pressure on minorities. Politicians whose minds were unable to disengage from the categories of the nation-state principle were only too prone to overlook the fact that the nation-states they cherished so much were also the product of historical development; that their territorial shape was moulded by the political constellations of the age, and frequently resulted from quite abstruse coincidences. If Tsarist Russia had not been repelled from East-Central Europe, for example, or if the Habsburg monarchy had not collapsed in 1918, Finland, the Baltic states, Poland and Czechoslovakia would hardly have been able to win independence at the end of the First World War.

Even the casual observer of European history since the French Revolution can see that the multitude of ethnic variations and distortions make it to all practical intents and purposes impossible for cultural nation and state perfectly to overlap. This is a universal problem faced by any nation-state order. It is at best possible to approximate to the ideal nation-state whose geographical size and domestic order are a direct function of the national homogeneity of its populace. Even the populations of the national states that have emerged in Western Europe generally include sizeable elements which speak a different language and may be called national minorities. Right up until the present day minorities have been the root of conflict between nations and nationalities, and the cause of irredentism in other states. This situation has generated a whole knot of problems to bedevil the history of modern Europe. Was it not ultimately a tragic error to dismiss the multinational state as a political anomaly?

The narrow nation-state perspective of much of modern historiography

---

[23] W. S. Churchill, *The Second World War*, vol. 1: *The Gathering Storm*, 9th ed., London 1971, p. 9.

is not so blinkered as to prevent recognition of the fact that the nation-state principle was never the only runner in the race. In terms of universal history, nation-states are the exception, even in the present and past centuries; multinational states are, in fact, the rule of historical reality. They still exist in present-day Europe, even after two hundred years of wrestling with national and nationalist issues, and national minorities have been expelled and resettled to and fro. In 'the age of the nation-state', Belgium, Romania, Switzerland and Russia clearly belong in the multinational camp. The regional movements in West and South-West Europe indicate, moreover, that Europe's old national states such as France or Spain are also essentially akin to cross-national polities. They merely deceived themselves into thinking they were nationally homogeneous 'historical' nations.[24]

We must hence conclude that the concept of the political nation, a major cornerstone of the great democratic countries of Western Europe, is only feasible under certain conditions. Put another way, the continuous process of nation-building has suffered a smarting blow in these states, for below the level of the political nation, linguistic, cultural and ethnic ties have been sustained, and in varying degrees have in recent years given rise to political movements. Empirical examination thus refutes the thesis that political nations and a liberal polity can eradicate ethnically based conflict. The individual relationship of loyalty that is the foundation of the political nation is, just like any other political and social structure, subject to change. Ernest Renan's dictum of the daily plebiscite that constitutes the nation also indicates that allegiance to a nation can be severed. Because of the dominance of subjective factors, the political concept of the nation can be criticized for allowing utilitarianism and opportunism; theoretically, membership of a nation can become a matter of convenience and political conformity. Proceeding from these criticisms, various arguments have been presented to show that the cultural concept of nation might be superior to a politically based definition, since it is based on objective criteria and hence far more stable, albeit not democratic. Whether this is accurate is open to debate.

Whatever the case, after appearing so resilient to the outside world for so long, the smooth façades of the centralist national states of Britain, France and Spain have crumbled. The only plausible conclusion to be drawn today is that even in modern Europe the nation-state inhabited by a unitary political nation was nothing but a theoretical scheme, a fictitious invention. As early as 1916, Ignaz Seipel, who was to become the Federal Chancellor of the first Austrian Republic, wrote: 'The nation-state seems only to be good as something after which one may strive; rarely can it be achieved, even for a short time, and it can never survive the long term. If it tries to maintain itself, it can do so only by resorting to an imperialism that denies the rights of other nations.'[25] It is, then, apparent that the

---

[24] James F. McMillan, *Twentieth-Century France. Politics and Society 1898–1991*, London 1992. Raymond Carr, *Spain 1808–1975*, 2nd ed., Oxford 1982.
[25] Ignaz Seipel, *Nation und Staat*, Vienna 1916, p. 15.

powerful ideology of the nation-state, even if related to the concept of the political nation, can only temporarily contain internal social fissures that result partly from historical coincidence and the deliberate, forcible integration which characterized the birth of that state. The backlash comes sooner or later.[26] So is the nation-state merely the intellectual edifice of revolutionary thinkers, impossible to build in political reality? Is the nation-state a myth?

The continued presence of multinational states in Europe is also a reminder that in a relatively large number of cases national states have failed to emerge, even though national movements have been feverishly active since the early nineteenth century. The image of an inexorable dynamism inherent in nationalism and the nation-state principle is clouded somewhat if we bear in mind that they were often stopped in their tracks. The specific constellation of nineteenth-century political forces denied the Scots and the Welsh national states, for instance. But while their ambitions were frustrated, the Irish, who likewise belonged to the United Kingdom, eventually won their battle after years of wrangling, violence and eventually revolution. The Basques and Catalans have been as hapless as the Scots and Welsh in winning their own states, though there is no denying the strength of national feeling they have been expressing for more than a hundred years. Similarly, Corsicans and Bretons have hitherto been refused their own states.[27] Only the future will reveal whether a solution will be found by the central governments in London, Madrid and Paris consenting to some of the demands of the 'unfulfilled' nationalisms (often euphemistically termed 'regionalism') alive in the outlying areas of their countries. Even after two hundred years of experience with nationalism and national movements the number of European nations and nation-states has not been settled for definite.

The European nation-state order has, however, remained very largely unaltered since it emerged at the end of the First World War, though it was temporarily disturbed in the 1930s by the expansionist axis powers, Germany and Italy. In 1945 the allied victors reversed the territorial changes imposed on the political map of Europe, such as the annexation of Austria and the Sudetenland by Nazi Germany in 1938, and the incorporation by Italy of Albania, Dalmatia and Slovenia in 1941. The territorial modifications brought about after the Soviet Union began its drive westwards following the Hitler–Stalin pact of 1939, were not reversed at the end of the war. The USSR retained Eastern Poland and the three Baltic states, which had been part of the Tsarist Empire before their period of independence, as well as Ruthenia, Northern Bukovina, Bessarabia and the northern parts of East Prussia, which Russia annexed at the end of the war. But neither these changes, nor the collapse of the German Reich and

---

[26] On the French example, see Brian Jenkins, *Nationalism in France. Class and Nation since 1789*, London 1990.

[27] Michael Watson (ed.), *Contemporary Minority Nationalism*, London 1990 (repr. 1992). Michael Keating, *State and Regional Nationalism. Territorial Politics and the European State*, Hemel Hempstead 1988.

its division into two states, shook the overall stability of the European nation-state order. A new order only emerged after the end of the communist regimes in Eastern Europe, and with the break-up of the Soviet Union, Yugoslavia and Czechoslovakia since 1990.

5 Decolonization

By 1918–19 and again after 1990, the nation-state idea had marched across Europe, but on the whole did not bear the fruits that idealist nineteenth-century nationalists had hoped for; their high-flown aspirations were confounded as it failed to herald an era of harmonious co-operation and political give-and-take between now self-determining nations. Mazzini's 'natural' order of states did not bring peace. The actions and thoughts of statesmen continued to centre on their own countries. Nation-states also turned out to be of limited benefit for civil liberties. People had once longed for the 'age of the nation-state'; in the twentieth century they were wont to heap scorn upon it, for it failed to rid the world of political rivalry and military conflict. This became apparent as early as the 'springtime of nations' in the 1848 Revolution. In the opinion of Lewis Namier, this same 'springtime of nations' dashed all hopes by unleashing 'the Great European War of every nation against its neighbours'.[28] In many respects the course of European history in the first half of the twentieth century can prompt no other conclusion than that the triumphal march of the nation-state has only taken tensions between European countries to unprecedented heights. As Europe lay divided and in ruins after 1945, the realization that this was the case was instrumental in thoroughly demolishing the rather naive faith in the pacificatory effects of the nation-state order.

The nation-state principle had not yet, however, relinquished every last claim to world-historical importance. But from the late 1940s onwards it did move to a new theatre of operations, the so-called Third World where it enjoyed a renaissance in the wake of the break-up of European colonial empires. The deluge of new states that emerged after 1945, almost without exception under the power of the nation-state ideal, reached such proportions that it made the gradual emergence of European state pluralism in the previous century pale into insignificance.

The white dominions of the British Empire can justly be regarded as the forerunners of decolonization, a world-historical process that paved the way for a radically new global order. Canada had been given the right to govern itself at a very early stage, when the British North America Act was passed in 1867. Australia followed in 1901, New Zealand in 1907, and the Union of South Africa in 1910. But these four dominions were still firmly tied to the British crown, and the British retained a voice in their foreign and defence policies. The last imperial authority of the British Parliament was not lifted until the Statute of Westminster in 1931. It is exceedingly difficult to say whether at this point the four dominions, all

---

[28] Namier, *Revolution of the Intellectuals*, p. 33.

of them colonies of expatriates, which obviously bore the mark of British society, became nation-states in the European sense of the term. The Union of South Africa certainly did not, for its population was divided into three large groups, Afrikaans-speaking Boers, the Britons who had immigrated since the nineteenth century (the 'uitlanders'), and the Blacks. The Boers at least regarded themselves as a nation with their own language and culture. With regard to Australia, the only nation that is a continent, the British historian Hugh Seton-Watson believes the Second World War to have been the decisive turning point, for an Australian national consciousness is in evidence only after the Japanese had threatened invasion, and following the wave of immigration, now mainly from continental Europe, that began shortly after 1945.[29]

The mandate system for former colonies of the German Reich and the Arab provinces of the Ottoman Empire is a further precursor of the Third World independence movement. After the Great War the newly formed League of Nations formally entrusted these territories to the European victor nations England, France and Belgium, and to Australia, New Zealand and the Union of South Africa. These countries had a brief to make suitable arrangements for their mandates' independence. When conditions were ripe for independence, and who would decide this, was left open. Only German South-West Africa (later Namibia) and the former German colonies in the Pacific were to be administered as integral parts of the territory of the mandatory powers. In principle, the mandate system was a transitional mechanism. Iraq, under British mandatory authority from 1921, gained sovereignty in 1932; the Lebanon and Syria, entrusted by the League to France, followed suit in 1943 and 1944 respectively, while Jordan bade farewell to British guidance in 1946 (see Table 4.2).

The Fourteen Points elaborated by the American President Woodrow Wilson, and the idea he sponsored of the League of Nations, gave only vague contours to a process that was really to take off after the Second World War, a conflict that also affected Asia and Africa: the break-up of the colonial empires. European colonies in South-East Asia had been partly occupied by Japanese forces during the war. The colonial peoples had made a major contribution to Allied victory over the Axis powers in the form of material and human resources. The price European colonialist powers would pay for their subjects' war effort was agreement to the demands of indigenous national movements, though they did so with hesitancy and reluctance. National feelings among colonial peoples were not novel; in British India, for instance, they had surfaced way back in the nineteenth century. Consequently it was across the Indian subcontinent that the first great wave of decolonization swept where four states – India, Pakistan, Ceylon and Burma – emerged after British withdrawal in 1947–48. Violent clashes and extensive population migration ensued before borders were finally fixed, especially between India and Pakistan, the latter being divided into a western and an eastern part (later Bangladesh).

---

[29] Hugh Seton-Watson, *Nations and States. An Enquiry into the Origins of Nations and the Politics of Nationalism*, London 1977, p. 236. See also S. Alomes, *A Nation at Last? The Changing Character of Australian Nationalism 1880–1988*, North Ryde 1988.

Table 4.2 Foundation of states since 1922 (year independence declared)

1922	Egypt
1932	Iraq, Saudi Arabia
1943	Lebanon
1944	Syria, Iceland
1946	Jordan, The Philippines, Mongolia
1947	India, Pakistan
1948	Burma (Myanmar), Ceylon (Sri Lanka), Israel, North Korea, South Korea
1949	Vietnam, Indonesia, German Democratic Republic, Federal Republic of Germany
1951	Libya
1954	Cambodia (Kampuchea), Laos
1956	Sudan, Morocco, Tunisia
1957	Ghana, Malaya (Malaysia since 1963)
1958	Guinea
1960	Cameroon, Senegal, Mali, Togo, Congo (Zaire), Madagascar, Somalia, Dahomey (Benin), Niger, Burkina Faso, Ivory Coast, Chad, Central African Republic, Congo (Brazzaville), Cyprus, Gabon, Nigeria, Mauritania
1961	Sierra Leone, Kuwait, Tanganyika (since 1964 Tanzania)
1962	Western Samoa, Burundi, Ruanda, Algeria, Jamaica, Trinidad and Tobago, Uganda
1963	Kenya
1964	Malawi, Malta, Zambia
1965	The Gambia, Maldives, Singapore
1966	Guyana, Botswana, Lesotho, Barbados
1968	Nauru, Mauritius, Swaziland, Equatorial Guinea, South Yemen
1970	Fiji, Oman, Tonga
1971	Bahrain, Bangladesh, Qatar, United Arab Emirates, Bhutan
1973	The Bahamas
1974	Grenada, Guinea-Bissau, Mozambique
1975	Angola, Cape Verde Islands, Sao Tomé and Principe, Surinam, Comoro Islands, Papua New Guinea
1976	Seychelles
1977	Djibouti
1978	Dominica, Solomon Islands, Tuvalu
1979	St Lucia, St Vincent, Kiribati
1980	Zimbabwe, Vanuatu
1981	Belize, Antigua and Barbuda
1983	St Kitts and Nevis
1984	Brunei
1986	Northern Mariana Islands
1990	Namibia, Micronesia, Marshall Islands, Armenia, Azerbaijan, Estonia, Georgia, Latvia, Lithuania
1991	Belarus, Kazakhstan, Kyrgyzstan, Moldova, Tajikistan, Turkmenistan, Ukraine, Uzbekistan, Bosnia-Herzegovina, Croatia, Macedonia, Slovenia
1993	Czech Republic, Slovakia, Eritrea

The principality of Kashmir was divided, with Pakistan and India both claiming the entire province as their own. In 1949, independence came to the two large regions of French and Dutch colonial rule in Asia (Indochina and Indonesia) after indigenous national liberation forces had thwarted a scheme to restore European colonial power after the war.

After 1956 the Third World independence movement spread to Africa.[30] Here the cause of national liberation won substantial popular support at a much later date than in Asia, in many cases not until after the Second World War. The Arab states of Sudan, Morocco and Tunisia started Africa's drive for sovereignty in 1956. Ghana, the ex-British Crown colony of the Gold Coast, became black Africa's first independent state in 1957. In early 1960 the British prime minister Harold Macmillan delivered a now-famous speech in Cape Town, in which he spoke of the 'wind of change' blowing across Africa: 'We have seen the awakening of national consciousness in peoples who have for centuries lived in dependence upon some other power. Fifteen years ago this movement spread through Asia . . . Today the same thing is happening in Africa, and the most striking of all the impressions I have formed since I left London a month ago is of the strength of this African national consciousness. In different places it takes different forms, but it is happening everywhere.'[31] 1960 has been quite rightly called 'Africa Year'. Within twelve months no fewer than 17 African states wrested sovereignty from the hands of their European colonial rulers (see Table 4.2). The most eloquent expression, both for Africans and the rest of the world, of this process, whose speed was unprecedented, was the membership list of the United Nations. The number of its members went up in leaps and bounds. The smallest of colonial territories, hitherto under the aegis of European power, now set out on the road to independence that could apparently no longer be blocked, and in doing so received effective political support from the growing UN majority of young states. The Organization of African Unity (OAU), founded in Addis Ababa in 1963, counted 51 members in 1984, 54 in 1993.

A mere cursory glance at the complicated political map of Africa is enough to justify talk of the territorial 'Balkanization' of that continent. In most cases, the shape of state territories originates directly from the arbitrary decisions of colonialists, who on the whole paid little heed to tribal allegiances or the ethnic and historic cohesion of different sections of the population. This notwithstanding, large and small African states alike see themselves as nation-states like the countries of Europe and Asia, occasionally with a disarming matter-of-factness. But in Africa, as in almost all of the developing world's younger states, there is a great discrepancy between claims and reality. Most of them have successfully managed the process of state-building, even if they have had to rely on one-party systems and military dictatorship as a last resort. But in many cases nation-building has not yet matured beyond infancy. The vast majority of young states in the Third World are states without nations,

---

[30] H. S. Wilson, *African Decolonization*, London 1993.
[31] Harold Macmillan, *Pointing the Way 1959–1961*, London 1972, p. 475.

and hence are not nation-states in the strict sense of the term. The concept of the nation-state describes a political programme in these states, not reality.[32] We shall return to this whole problem later.

6 Is the Nation-State an Anachronism?

Various features of the way in which the late twentieth-century world is arranged into states and peoples have promoted inquiry into whether the traditional nation-state that is the foundation of the current order can continue to be a suitable form of political organization in the present and future. Europe is still divided into nation-states; there is uncertainty about whether the political structure and economies of the increasing number of small and medium-sized states throughout the world can survive; at the same time, peoples and large social groups that perceive themselves as nations – Basques, Sikhs, Kurds, Tibetans for instance – are arbitrarily denied their own states. Is the autonomous nation-state as it actually exists today, and as it probably will exist in the future, capable of achieving what was hoped of it by its supporters in this and the last century? Will the hold it clearly continues to have over the political mind of ordinary citizens gradually begin to weaken? Have the political situation across the world, global economic constraints and the frightening advances of military technology not consigned it to history? Is the nation-state, in other words, an outdated relic of the past?

We have to look to the Europe of the late eighteenth and nineteenth centuries to find the intellectual roots of the nation-state. About that there can be no doubt. The nation-state was the offspring of nationalism, the idea of the nation and bourgeois liberalism. 'Genuine' nation-states tended to be the exception, however, in the ensuing period even in Europe. But an uninterrupted series of attempts to make fiction reality has caused the number of formally sovereign states in the world since then to spiral upwards. The United Nations Charter recognizes as legally binding the 'sovereign equality' of all its members, irrespective of their territorial extent, population, and economic and military might. Without question, however, the much-cited sovereign equality is more of a legislative principle than a reflection of political reality, for only a handful of leading powers are able to play a definitive and truly independent part on the world political stage today. Even in the case of so-called superpowers, the extent to which they can take autonomous decisions is highly disputed.

While the nation-state might appear to be an obsolete idea in some respects, its continuing validity is no doubt a fundamental reason why endeavours to unite separate states into supranational entities founder upon seemingly intractable difficulties. Be this as it may, there are currently signs at most of intensified regional co-operation between states, and of the subordination of many countries to the political, economic or ideological hegemony of a world power, i.e., of an involuntary decline

---

[32] Clifford Geertz, 'After the Revolution: The Fate of Nationalism in the New States', in: *idem, The Interpretation of Cultures. Selected Essays*, New York 1973, pp. 234–54.

in national state sovereignty. It would, however, be incorrect to conclude that these trends, which are of course more pronounced in some cases than others, amount to the erosion, let alone the disappearance, of conceptualization in terms of the nation-state. The world has not yet entered a post-national age.

Nevertheless, it can often be heard in political and academic debate that the nation-state is antiquated and can no longer be regarded as a legitimate form of political organization; that it is anachronistic as a referential framework for political and social existence. On returning from exile in America, in 1953 the German historian Hans Rothfels declared that after the experience of the two world wars and the perversion of the national idea by the totalitarian state, the 'dimensions of contemporary events' proved the 'crisis of the nation-state'; it was, in other words, 'dubious whether it can be a generally desirable goal any longer'.[33] Though Rothfels was sensitive to the first signs of decolonization in the Third World, events in East-Central Europe in the twentieth century led him to deem the sovereign nation-state an 'outdated, even reactionary form of life' because it had brought about 'the breakdown of economic and cultural ties and the excesses of nationalism'.[34] The task now at hand was to devise new modes of human co-existence – arrangements that would replace or by-pass the nation-state. The hegemony of the nation-state and its totalist claim on the individual could be escaped only by recognizing that nation and nation-state were concepts embedded in a particular age. If only thought could be diverted from the nation-state and reorientated around a more sensible parameter, the co-existence of nations and nationalities in Europe and elsewhere could start to be restructured on federalist and autonomist principles.

In a very similar vein, the constitutional jurist Ulrich Scheuner has underscored that the nation-state has been rooted in European history since the French Revolution, and that the perception of the nation-state is decisively shaped by a cultural consciousness unique to the nation and by territorial aspirations combined with historical experience. Outside Europe, the nation-state idea is, according to Scheuner, not so deeply anchored; here its significance is merely as a signpost to the future, a principle that 'seeks to consolidate polities that have emerged under different conditions'.[35] Like Rothfels, Scheuner also regards the nation-state of European provenance as obsolete, because it relates to a specific period and specific historical circumstances. The only reason the nation-state order in Europe was restored in such an otherwise unwarranted manner after 1945 was because the victorious Allies explicitly intended so to do. The need for an 'overarching international order', however, will in the future cause the nation-state principle increasingly to wither away.[36]

---

[33] Hans Rothfels, 'Zur Krise des Nationalstaats', in: *idem*, *Zeitgeschichtliche Betrachtungen*, 2nd ed., Goettingen 1963, pp. 124 and 138.

[34] *Ibid.*, p. 131.

[35] Ulrich Scheuner, 'Nationalstaatsprinzip und Staatenordnung seit dem Beginn des 19. Jahrhunderts', in: Theodor Schieder/Peter Alter (eds), *Staatsgründungen und Nationalitäts-prinzip*, Munich 1974, p. 10.

[36] *Ibid.*, p. 11.

There are of course also many who disagree with such predictions. They argue that the nation-state principle will retain its centrality to human co-existence because, as they rightly point out, a convincing alternative to the current basis of the world order has yet to be found. Whether the nation-state is still a valid political unit has, then, to be an open question. There can be no doubt, however, that international communication structures are becoming more complex, that the world economic system is spreading further and further, and that the borders of national states are now more penetrable than ever. The late twentieth century is witnessing the earliest stages of something akin to a transnational, global society that has been breaking the political, economic, cultural and military autarchy of nation-states (if such ever existed).

As a consequence of the freer movement of individuals, goods and capital, internationalization has left nation-states but marginal scope to intervene in their economic affairs. International bodies like the United Nations, the World Bank and the European Union (European Community until November 1993) are performing functions that used to be essentially the responsibility of individual states. These bodies were created in response to needs that could never have been satisfied within the nation-state framework. Today even ordinary people are well aware that in the age of advanced industrialization, economic crises and environmental pollution problems do not respect national frontiers. Moreover, awareness that modern weapons technology and the global nuclear threat mean that practically no country on earth can now provide even minimal security for its borders without wide-scale defence systems, has become part and parcel of everyday international politics.

However, none of this should tempt us to forget that, despite every endeavour since the Second World War to set up forms of supranational co-operation in certain fields and at regional levels, the nation-state still plays an important role in political and social life. As far as the individual is concerned, it remains the basic point of reference for socio-economic development; it is still entrusted with the maintenance of domestic and social peace, and for upholding the rule of law. As the framework of the political, legal and social order, the nation-state penetrates deep into the lives of its citizens. In the opinion of Karl Deutsch, it 'offers most of its members a stronger sense of security, belonging or affiliation, and even personal identity, than does any alternative large group'. Deutsch goes on to say that the 'greater the need of the people for such affiliation and identity under the strains and shocks of social mobilization and alienation from earlier familiar environments, the greater becomes the potential power of the nation-state to channel both their longings and resentments and to direct their love and hate.' It is for this reason that nation-states have become more powerful and more numerous since 1945, while international organizations, 'despite their impressive growth, thus far have remained so much weaker'.[37]

---

[37] Deutsch, 'Nation and World', in: Ithiel de Sola Pool (ed.), *Contemporary Political Science: Toward Empirical Theory*, New York 1967, p. 217.

The dilemma facing nation-states today has been widely recognized. While they are undeniably still interested in securing their sovereignty and territorial integrity as firmly as ever, they find they are forced to join larger economic, political and ideological communities merely to ensure survival. Yet those who predicted at the end of the Second World War that the end of the nation-state was nigh have all been proved wrong, for the 'nation-state' and its ideology are apparently indispensable to contemporary mankind. This is true as much of America, Asia and Africa as it is of Europe. Indeed, experience *vis-à-vis* the young states of the Third World and Eastern Europe confirms the assumption that the nation-state is an apparently necessary stage in the development of a body politic. But it is nonetheless doubtful whether the nation-state is still really capable of playing the role generally expected of it.

The conclusion to be drawn is that the idealized state entity, founded upon a linguistically, culturally and ethnically homogeneous nation, is incapable of promoting more peaceful co-existence between peoples. Quite the opposite tends to be the case. The route which has taken almost all peoples of the world to the freedom of their formally independent states has also led to a growth in the scenarios of possible conflict. Tensions once felt within one large state have now often been raised to the level of international conflicts. But the new multitude of nation-states has simultaneously proved impotent to resolve these rapidly mounting problems.[38]

In some respects then, the traditional nation-state is unsuited to modern conditions, and deserves to be labelled anachronistic. This does not mean, however, that it should be simply abolished, nor that international economic and political integration should equate with a surrender of national identity (and multiplicity) for those involved. The choice for the present and immediate future cannot be a crude alternative between either unconditional affirmation of the nation-state in its traditional form and function, or swift replacement of it by supranational institutions. A middle way is conceivable, though one that can be only imprecisely formulated at this stage: in order to facilitate their continued presence in a new world order, nation-states could acquire a redefined form and function by gradually transferring to supranational bodies some of the tasks they have hitherto administered. The nation-state which has voluntarily dispensed with the claim to absolute sovereignty in all matters and to the supreme loyalty of its citizens may, after all, retain its political and social significance in the next century.

---

[38] Anthony Giddens, *The Nation-State and Violence*, Cambridge 1985.

5

The Renaissance of Nationalism

I Nationalism and the Nation in Post-War Europe

The crisis or, rather, the uncertain future of the nation-state may be seen
as one of the most eloquent signs that, in Europe at least, the nation's
absolute claim to loyalty has been eroded. By 1945 the attraction and
legitimacy of national ideology had suffered a tremendous blow. In the
first major study of nationalism to appear in German after the war, Eugen
Lemberg remarked in 1950 that 'there is a general feeling in Europe that
we are bidding farewell to an epoch.' With Europe's recent experience fresh
in his mind, he set out to analyse and fathom 'one of the most mysterious
puzzles of our age'.[1]

Lord Acton's criticism of nationalism and the nation-state, dismissed as
untimely by those around him who had faith in its Risorgimento traditions, now appeared in quite a different light, particularly to West Europeans. All the evidence suggested that while the majority of Europeans,
who had been witness to nationalist zealotry on an inconceivable scale,
did not entirely write nationalism off, they had now acquired a more
measured attitude to it. But this certainly did not mean that national
identity had become irrelevant. An accurate term has yet to be found
to describe the 'normal', legitimate variety of nationalism common in
Western Europe today, as opposed to both the Risorgimento and integral
types we have been discussing. Everyday English might refer to it as 'a
sense of national pride', while a German would call it 'robust national feeling'. Those who share this feeling regard the nation and the national
interest neither as subordinate to other values and goals, nor as the
exclusive yardstick for their thought and actions; religion, humanity, and
truth are equally valid. 'Moderate nationalism' might perhaps best encap-
sulate the essence of this phenomenon, or the somewhat old-fashioned
concept of 'patriotism'.

When the war ended, the European countries that had been occupied
and annexed by Nazi Germany were restored,[2] which on the face of it
seemed like a direct return to the state order of 1918–19. But the conviction

---

[1] Eugen Lemberg, *Geschichte des Nationalismus in Europa*, Stuttgart 1950, pp. 9 and 5.
[2] Alan S. Milward, *The European Rescue of the Nation-State*, London 1992, esp. pp. 21–45.

was now widespread, particularly in Western Europe, that the sovereignty of nation-states in the old sense must yield to greater international coalescence. The common experience of Nazi dictatorship, and the destruction and desolation that engulfed almost the entire continent had given enormous impetus to the idea of European unity, an idea that resistance movements in various European countries had fanned even as that war had raged. Fear of communism and Soviet expansion, of which Czechoslovakia had become the latest victim in February 1948, cleared the ground even more for west European integration. The broad outline of a policy of unity began to surface after 1950, with the Schuman Plan in 1951, and the creation of the European Coal and Steel Community in the following year.[3] Initially the European policy of integration concerned only the core states of France, Italy, the Benelux countries and the Federal Republic of Germany that had emerged in 1949 from the bankruptcy of the German Reich, but the long-term aim was a supranational United Europe. In his famous speech in Zurich on 19 September 1946 Winston Churchill had already spoken of the desirability and necessity of such.[4] Nothing definite was said of whether and to what extent this European project would one day include the countries under Soviet influence in East-Central and South-East Europe.

Structural shifts in the world economy and the long period of sustained growth since the 1950s have also caused nationalism to wane in the industrialized states of Western Europe. 'Capitalist internationalism', reflected in the growth of multinational companies, has continued to spread more or less undisturbed, despite some nationalist backlashes against it. Propitious economic conditions after 1950 in more prosperous countries such as West Germany have meant that conflicts over the distribution of the national product had become less heated, and were no longer fought out at the level of ideology. This contrasted sharply with the situation after 1918. In West Germany, for example, general post-war affluence, under the popular slogan of 'wealth for all', went hand in hand with the integration of the working classes into the social and political system,[5] and obviated the deep-seated fears of downward social mobility which had made the middle classes so sympathetic to National Socialism in the critical years after 1929.

Endeavours to bring about the economic, and ultimately political, integration of Western Europe, a project which lost some of its initial dynamism in the 1970s following the successes of the 1950s and 60s, were in retrospect the most tangible expression of changed European attitudes to nationalism. The virulent irredentist tendencies that had dominated the continent's history since the late nineteenth century, reaching a climax between the wars, had become the exception after 1945. This was partly

---

[3] William Diebold, *The Schuman Plan. A Study in Economic Cooperation 1950–1959*, New York 1959.

[4] See Walter Lipgens, *A History of European Integration*, vol. 1: 1945–47, Oxford 1982, pp. 317–23.

[5] Alan Kramer, *The West German Economy, 1945–1955*, New York 1991. Hans-Joachim Braun, *The German Economy in the Twentieth Century: The German Reich and the Federal Republic*, London 1990.

connected with the fact that the nationality problems in East-Central Europe, particularly in Poland, had been simplified, if not entirely resolved, during and after the war by forcible expulsions and resettlements. Most West and all East European states were, moreover, embraced by superpower-led alliances whose overriding political purposes allowed little scope for irredentist aspirations.

The Republic of Ireland has been the only country in post-war Western Europe to harbour territorial ambitions: towards the north-eastern part of the island that, under the name Northern Ireland, remained part of the United Kingdom when Southern Ireland gained independence in 1921–22. The southern Irish claims, which are vehemently rejected by the majority in the north, are founded on the belief that Irish geographical and national unity must be identical. It should not be forgotten, however, that the Dublin government has in recent years dropped the demand for Irish reunification, with the result that little energy has been devoted to the question of how a merger might actually take place. Both the Irish and British governments increasingly acknowledge the need to solve the long-standing problem of Northern Ireland within a wider, innovative framework that leaves nineteenth-century approaches and nationalist thinking well behind.[6]

The notion that the Federal Republic of Germany had revisionist and revanchist designs on ex-German territories east of the Oder-Neisse line had since the 1960s been nothing but a story trumped up by the Soviet propaganda machine. By highlighting alleged German ambitions, the Soviets had an instrument which could be easily used to integrate Soviet Eastern Europe and counteract the desires of the peoples living there for greater national and political independence. Treaties with Poland and Czechoslovakia which the West German government signed in the early 1970s and confirmed in the negotiations leading up to German unification in 1990 finally laid this issue to rest.

Early hopes and schemes notwithstanding, the politics of west European unity have thus far failed to alter the continent's basic nation-state structure. The notion of state pluralism is rooted more deeply here than perhaps anywhere in the world. The Western Europe of the 1990s is further away from political unity than the leaders of the early days, such as Robert Schuman, Jean Monnet, Alcide de Gasperi, Konrad Adenauer and Paul Henri Spaak would have expected; the Europeanism so exciting in the early 1950s has now dwindled. Since Soviet-type communism is no longer felt to pose a direct threat, nationalism has undergone a limited renaissance, even in the member states of the European Union. But it has been no more than limited because the overwhelming majority of West Europeans no longer subscribe to the kind of nationalism characterized by exclusive identification with one's own nation. This is a thing of the past. The major reasons why European unification has stagnated must be sought in the fact that countries have objected to restrictions on their national sovereignty, and given priority to their own national interests in tackling pressing social

---

[6] John McGarry/Brendan O'Leary (eds), *The Future of Northern Ireland*, Oxford 1990.

and economic problems. France and the United Kingdom in particular have all too frequently been guilty of resorting to a policy of national egoism. The de Gaullean tactic of strictly upholding sovereignty and national prestige served not least to make the loss of France's extensive colonial territory in Asia and Africa during the 1960s easier to bear, and to blur serious social and regional conflict at home.

While criticism can quite justifiably be levelled at the pace and state of European integration in the closing years of the twentieth century, at the seemingly sterile and blown-up bureaucratism of the Brussels Commission, and the readiness of member states to pursue their national concerns, the Union has engendered a degree of co-operation unparalleled in Western Europe's modern history. For ordinary citizens it has meant substantial economic gains, and made life enormously simpler in areas such as travel, choice of job and place of residence. Frontiers in Western Europe now no longer tend to isolate people from one another. This extraordinary porousness is taken for granted, especially by the younger generations who only have history books to tell them of the Europe of old, torn and devastated by national antagonism and war. The contrast is brought out vividly by comparison with conditions in other parts of the world.

The importance of nationalist currents or undercurrents in the countries of Western Europe varies from one to another. However, resurgence of extreme forms of nationalism is visible everywhere at the end of the twentieth century; it is now probably the greatest threat to liberal democracy since communism. Right-wing and racist parties are successful in local, regional, national and European elections not only in France, Belgium and Germany, but also in Austria, Italy and Britain. Nationalist groups and associations demonstrate openly. They try to popularize their backward-looking and rather woolly message, which in many cases simply boils down to identifying scapegoats for social, political and economic problems. Since the early 1990s, in Germany, France and Britain ethnic minorities and immigrants have come under attack by hooligans and neo-Nazis. They justify their criminal acts by appealing to the so-called interest of the nation. They adhere to the old Darwinian belief that all nations are caught up in an animal struggle for survival, and interpret it in their own simplistic way. In Germany the slogan is '*Ausländer raus*' ('foreigners out'), in France supporters of the National Front warn of the Arab 'invasion' of France, and in the United Kingdom the British National Party blames immigrants from the Indian subcontinent for the housing shortage in the East End of London. Even in a country like Sweden where overt nationalism had long been a taboo, the advertising of 'Swedishness' has become almost commonplace. As elsewhere in Europe, in Stockholm and towns across the country small but highly visible neo-Nazi groups could be seen cropping up to taunt immigrants, scrawling 'Sweden for the Swedes' on walls and rubbish bins.

These may seem to be rather primitive expressions of xenophobia, racism and nationalist insights into the structure and working of society. But, at the same time, they readily provide a clue to an understanding of the underlying causes of extremist nationalism and racist policies as advocated by the nationalist far-right. Once again, extreme nationalism is the product of political, social and economic upheavals. The global economic crisis since the late 1980s, high unemployment, de-industrialization, the formation of a new underclass of anxious citizens, the influx of dramatically growing numbers of refugees and 'asylum-seekers' from the Third World,[7] confrontation with 'otherness', resentment at the deficiencies of parliamentary democracy – all these factors provide the breeding-ground for nationalist demagogy and electioneering.

The danger of extreme nationalists breaking into local and national politics is, with the possible exception of France, greatest in unified Germany. In 1992 Germany witnessed a surge of racism which saw a number of people killed and more than 2,000 acts of violence related to right-wing extremism. A very large majority of the persons committing acts of extremist or racist violence were juveniles or young adults. Government statistics show that almost 70 per cent of suspects identified were under twenty years of age, and only 2 per cent over thirty.[8] All this came as a shock, because after the unprecedented catastrophes of their recent history and the collapse of a national state that had not been created until 1871, Germans had understandably distanced themselves from their traditional nationalist concepts much more than other Europeans. Post-war West German society was indeed marked for a long time by strong anti-national leanings. It compensated for the enforced division of the nation with resolute commitment to Europe as a kind of surrogate nation; West Germans replaced old national ideology with the new idea of European unity. In resolutely re-orienting their political agenda, they were only a small step behind their neighbours in the Benelux countries.

With the exception of obscure right-wing extremist groups, and the ephemeral political importance of parties like the National Democratic Party of Germany (NPD), an organized, mass-based nationalist movement has not emerged since the West German state was founded in 1949. This was all the more remarkable if we consider that the loss of the eastern territories of Silesia, Pomerania and East Prussia, and the division of the rest of Germany could easily have spurred such developments. The millions of immigrants and refugees from formerly German areas, various east European states and the German Democratic Republic (GDR), the former Soviet zone of occupation, provided an enormous reservoir of potential support for a nationalist backlash. Helped by the salubrious impact of the post-war economic boom and continued prosperity, one of the greatest achievements of the West German republic is to have integrated these people into economic, political and social life.

Since the 1970s supposed signs of a new German nationalism had occasionally been hyperbolized. This could to a certain extent be regarded as a reaction to the rejuvenation of interest in the national question in Germany. There has been a flurry of writing on this long-ignored subject. The more the Federal Republic was consolidated as a state, and the more

---

[7] In 1992 nearly 450,000 people entered Germany as 'asylum-seekers' and immigrants (*Guardian* 9 March 1993).

[8] Embassy of the Federal Republic of Germany, London, report, 14 January 1993, p. 4.

it lost the provisional character with which it was initially endowed, the more animated debate on 'German identity' and German political consciousness became. West Germany's provisional status had come to an end by December 1972 at the latest, when the Basic Treaty was signed with East Germany (GDR). Hardly anyone doubted that, after so many years of division, the two German states that resulted from defeat in 1945, Allied occupation and the Cold War, had each generated a state consciousness. They were related to the respective political system and specific social order. The thesis that the two successor states on the soil of the former German Reich had each developed a separate national consciousness overstated the case, however, and was, all things considered, inaccurate. Some observers went so far as to call West Germany a 'post-national democracy' whose citizens were expected to show 'constitutional patriotism' – that is, a sort of enthusiasm for the constitution (the 'basic law') of 1949.[9]

In spite of the consolidation of the two German successor states, reunification of the divided country remained one of the main political objectives of the Federal Republic. This stance was emphatically backed by the Western allies who, in 1952, when the formal occupation of Western Germany was about to end, firmly pledged to support a common goal: 'a reunified Germany enjoying a liberal-democratic constitution like that of the Federal Republic, and integrated within the European community.'[10] Exactly this was achieved 38 years later when the unification of Germany quite unexpectedly came about in October 1990 after the pathetic collapse of the GDR.

In the years prior to unification on Western terms, the communist regime in East Germany also carried on using national categories and the national ideology for quite obvious reasons. Since the early 1970s the German communists had been pushing the notion of a 'socialist German nation' supposedly in existence in East Germany which, it was said, had nothing to do with the 'capitalist nation' in the Federal Republic.[11] The reasoning was simple: the Cold War after 1945 had produced two German states, the German nation had been split and, as a natural corollary, had given way to two new nations which were not based on cultural identity, social communication, shared values or any other traditional criteria, but solely on social class. The political reality of a 'socialist nation' would have strengthened enormously the communist state in the East.

Despite many efforts to propagate the concept of a 'socialist nation' in East Germany, there was in fact no evidence whatsoever that it had gained political momentum outside the dream world of government circles in East Berlin. It was a negation of reality to assume that the nation could be based

---

[9] John Ardagh, *Germany and the Germans*, London 1987, pp. 447–59. Gordon A. Craig, *The Germans*, New York 1982, pp. 289–309.

[10] 'Convention on Relations between the Three Powers and the Federal Republic of Germany', article 7, 26 May 1952, in: *British Foreign Policy: Some Relevant Documents, January 1950–April 1955*, London and New York 1955, p. 113.

[11] Klaus Beyme, 'National Consciousness and Nationalism: The Case of the Two Germanies', in: *Canadian Review of Studies in Nationalism* 13 (1986), pp. 227–48.

on a political and economic order which had existed for just forty years and was far from being accepted by the people. This assumption collapsed like a hot-air balloon pricked by a needle when the mounting stream of mostly young East German refugees fleeing to the Federal Republic via Hungary and Czechoslovakia, harbingers of dramatic developments to come, turned into a flood after August 1989. Their departure was a devastating vote of no confidence in the hard-line communist leadership of their country and in the validity of the so-called German Democratic Republic itself. The extraordinary events which surrounded the opening of the Berlin Wall in November 1989, and the mass demonstrations in East German cities demanding democracy, freedom and German unity were the symbolic funeral of the 'socialist German nation'.

Unification itself had very little to do with nationalism, let alone chauvinism – but much to do with joy and relief that the East Germans, after almost sixty years of Nazi and communist dictatorship, had at last regained their political freedom and were able to join a democratic Europe which is irrevocably set on course towards closer co-operation. The outbursts of racist nationalism after unification should not be allowed to darken out of all proportion the overall picture of a democratic and non-nationalist Germany. They must be seen as an integral part of a common European trend in recent years, which is as deplorable as it is despicable. And it must also be borne in mind that nationalist activities in Germany after unification appear to be confined to small segments of the population.[12] However, a close watch will have to be kept on whether extreme nationalism, which inevitably conjures up an evil past, succeeds in leaving the political ghetto and is able to infect broader sections of German society with its primitive message.

2 Regionalism in Western Europe

It is not only extreme forms of nationalism that continue to plague Europe in the closing years of the twentieth century. Claims by national minorities for more autonomy, national separatism of the kind Europe faced in the nineteenth century, and other nation-related problems still exist in varying shapes and sizes even in the age of (Western) European union. And however dominant the nation and national identification, individuals and groups retain a multiplicity of allegiances which may compete with loyalty to the distinctive nation and its state. Individuals live happily with a number of identifications and are used to moving between them as the situation requires. They identify themselves with a family, a town, a region, a nation, or a gender, a class, a religion – it all depends on context,

---

[12] Jost Halfmann, 'From Defeat to Demise: German Nationalism at the End of the Twentieth Century', in: *History of European Ideas* 15 (1992), pp. 817–25. Dieter Grosser (ed.), *German Unification: The Unexpected Challenge*, Oxford 1992. Thomas Saalfeld, 'The Politics of National-Populism: Ideology and Policies of the German Republikaner Party', in: *German Politics* 2 (1993), pp. 177–99.

sentiment and frame of reference.[13] As was true on the political level more than a century ago, the key to the solution lies in striking a balance between the demands of regions or national minorities for political, economic and social equality and the need to preserve the integrity and cohesion of the nation-state.

Confronted with the revival of regional consciousness and the demands of hitherto dormant ethnic communities, Belgium has been the most resolute of all the West European countries in reacting to the challenge that at times has threatened to destroy its unity. A comprehensive reform of government in 1980 transformed Belgium from a centrally ruled unitary state into a federation largely allowing not only the Flemings and the Walloons but also the German-speaking minority in Eupen and Malmédy in east Belgium the right to run their own affairs. In Cyprus, another country in modern Europe where nationalism has lost none of its explosive power, the provisions that were meant to guarantee equal rights for Greeks and Turks when the island became independent in 1960 have failed in practice. The two communities split in February 1975, and it seems most unlikely that a new constitution can ultimately reverse the political division of the island.

Since the 1960s even the west European countries that are normally regarded as the very model of modern centralist nation-states, founded upon the concept of the political nation – the 'historic' nation-states such as Spain, France or Britain – have been faced with the aspirations and ideals of coherent social groups which either regard themselves as national minorities or are conscious of their ethnic and cultural specificity. It is the question of regionalism: resistance to the state's centre from peripheral areas. There is no general agreement on the underlying causes of regionalism, though in many cases it is clearly linked to earlier, interrupted attempts to create national states. But there is no doubting its political significance as yet further proof of the crisis of the nation-state and its loss of integrative power in Europe. Like the idea of European unity, regionalism seems to signal the end of the age of homogeneous and allegedly independent nation-states. On the one hand, nation-states have come under external pressure to delegate some major areas of economic and socio-political responsibility to overarching supranational institutions such as the European Union; on the other, they have run up against demands at home for the decentralization of political and economic power.

From a wider perspective, the regionalism now alive in France, Italy, Spain and Britain eloquently demonstrates that these 'political nations' never were completely united and homogeneous. Here too, state-building and nation-building were two different things that neither ran on the same time-scale nor registered equal results. Even these countries have obviously failed to fulfil three of the conditions requisite for a successful political system: the political and cultural identity of the population; a

[13] Anthony D. Smith, 'National Identity and the Idea of European Unity', in: *International Affairs* 68 (1992), pp. 55–72.

high degree of allegiance to the centre; and the acceptance of shared political aims.[14] The breeding-ground for regionalism in centralist nation-states is provided by the continuing presence of both economic hetero-geneity and cultural and linguistic disparity. Welsh, for example, is still spoken by approximately one-fifth of the population of Wales who, like the Scots, have a distinctive cultural consciousness. In Spain, the only time the special ethnic and cultural characteristics of Basques and Catalans were denied was during the Franco era (1939–75) when they were brutally sup-pressed. In France, most Bretons, Corsicans, Alsatians and Provençals speak a second language that is different from French. Nevertheless all French political parties reject the idea that France can be called a multina-tional state: according to the French concept of the nation any inhabitant with French citizenship is French. In the French perspective this rules out the possibility of equating regionalism with nationalism, and dismisses any understanding of regionalism based on certain cultural and linguistic peculiarities and on economic grievances as a new nationalism 'from below'.

It is extremely problematic to argue unequivocally that as a matter of principle it is wrong to treat regionalist movements as nationalist. That the emergence of nations over the last two hundred years has created smaller political entities (with the exception of Italy and Germany in the nineteenth century) cannot be questioned. Logically then, one might claim, regionalist movements are merely the continuation of this general pattern since they aim to decentralize power and change the shape of large polities. But does this mean that regionalist forces essentially hope to form political units that will eventually break away from the greater body? Large social groups which, recognizing they have certain characteristics in common, feel they constitute a nation and insist on the right to political self-determination, foster national movements. Their goal is a sovereign national state, and they frequently regard political autonomy within a disintegrating multinational state as a transitional stage on the way to full independence. So, do regionalists and nationalists, after all, have identical goals?

If we examine the manifestos and declarations of the parties and other bodies that constitute regionalist movements, we gain an ambiguous pic-ture. In Spain, where the most powerful of such pressures in Western Europe are at work, only Catalan and Basque regionalism have ever managed to rise to political significance.[15] But, after the end of the Franco regime, similar movements came to the surface in other parts of the country too. Local Catalan feeling has enjoyed fluctuating support ever since the nineteenth century, and has only rarely receded entirely. Though some fringe groups demand secession from Spain, the general aim of the movement is to bring about extensive cultural and political autonomy for

---

[14] Stein Rokkan, 'Center Formation, Nation-Building, and Cultural Diversity', in: S. N. Eisenstadt/S. Rokkan (eds), *Building States and Nations*, Beverly Hills (Calif.) 1973, pp. 17–20.

[15] Jean Grugel, 'The Basques', in: Michael Watson (ed.), *Contemporary Minority Nationalism*, London 1992, pp. 100–16.

Catalonia within the wider state. Such autonomy was accorded between 1932 and 1939 by the Second Spanish Republic, and reinstituted by the new constitution of 1979, which defines Spain as a multi-cultural country and grants regional self-government to the 'nationalities'. Other regions also took advantage of the new rulings. There are now 17 autonomous regions.[16]

Central government concessions bringing about autonomy satisfied all except the Basques, whose separatism is voiced not only by radical organizations such as the Herri Batasuna Party ('Unity of the People') and ETA (Euskadi ta Askatasuna – 'Basque Homeland and Liberty'), formed in 1959, but also by the local ruling Basque Nationalist Party (Partido Nacionalista Vasco – PNV). Though the autonomy granted to the Basques by the central government in Madrid in 1979 is relatively generous, they regard it as no more than an interim solution. In the Spanish general election of June 1993 the PNV gained a disappointing 1.24 per cent of the total vote (five seats in the Madrid parliament), Herri Batasuna only 0.88 per cent (two seats). The PNV's and ETA's ultimate goal is to unite the three Spanish Basque provinces of Guipúzcoa, Vizcaya and Alava with the three Basque *arrondissements* of Basses-Pyrénées in South-West France, and the Spanish region of Navarra, the north of which is inhabited by Basques. With a population of three million, the seven 'Basque Provinces' would be joined in an independent state.

It is unclear whether French Basques are sympathetic to this plan; if they are, they have yet to demonstrate their feelings in an organized manner. The Bretons and the Corsicans, both of whom have a long historical tradition, have been the major sources of regionalism in France, the many varieties of which have, at least in public, been more concerned about cultural rather than political autonomy. Political separatism seems to have been a central plank in Breton regionalism only in its early stages, in the years before the First World War. When it re-emerged in the mid-1960s its methods of agitation and the names of its organizations – Breton Liberation Front, Breton Revolutionary Army – were decidedly more radical than was its political programme. The same is true of Corsica, where some groups use terrorism and violence to back up their demands; these do not, however, include insistence on an independent Corsican state. In the 1980s 'autonomist' parties won around 15 per cent of the vote in regional elections.

Like their Corsican counterparts, Welsh and Scottish regionalist organizations are not too serious about complete political separation. In the mid-1970s fears that the United Kingdom of Great Britain and Northern Ireland was about to 'break up' were widely aired;[17] but this was as unreal a danger then as it is now, and will be in the foreseeable future. In this sense, the situation in Britain and France is unlike that in Spain. The best-known organization in Wales is Plaid Cymru, founded in 1925, and in Scotland the Scottish National Party, formed in 1934. Occasionally

---

[16] See Michael Keating, *State and Regional Nationalism. Territorial Politics and the European State*, Hemel Hempstead 1988, pp. 97–108, 211–30.

[17] Tom Nairn, *The Break-Up of Britain. Crisis and Neo-Nationalism*, London 1977.

Table 5.1 How the Scottish National Party has fared in general elections since 1959

	Number of votes	Number of candidates	% of Scottish vote	Seats
1959	21,738	5	0.8	0
1964	64,044	15	2.4	0
1966	128,474	23	5.0	0
1970	306,802	65	11.4	0
1974 (Feb.)	632,032	70	21.9	7
1974 (Oct.)	839,628	71	30.4	11
1979	504,259	71	17.3	2
1983	331,975	71	16.3	2
1987	409,970	71	14.0	3
1992	629,564	72	21.5	3

Table 5.2 How Plaid Cymru has fared in general elections since 1959

	Number of votes	Number of candidates	% of Welsh vote	Seats
1959	77,571	20	5.2	0
1964	69,507	23	4.8	0
1966	61,071	20	4.3	0
1970	175,016	36	11.5	0
1974 (Feb.)	171,634	36	10.7	2
1974 (Oct.)	166,321	36	10.8	3
1979	132,544	36	8.1	2
1983	125,309	36	7.8	2
1987	133,589	38	7.3	3
1992	154,947	38	8.9	4

resorting to militancy, Scottish and Welsh regionalism represent minority movements, though they are sometimes popular among the voters in general and local elections (see Tables 5.1 and 5.2). While such successes are always exaggerated by the British media as signs of the potency and putative threat of regionalism,[18] it should nevertheless be remembered that the SNP is, behind Labour, the second-strongest party in many Scottish constituencies.

The Northern Ireland problem, by contrast, places a severe strain on the British state, and is of a quite different order to Anglo-Scottish and Anglo-Welsh tensions. It is not a matter of regionalism. Two-thirds of the one-and-a-half million inhabitants of Northern Ireland have a deep emotional attachment to the mainland, the original home of their migrant ancestors centuries ago. 'Protestant' and 'Catholic', crucial terms of differentiation in Northern Ireland, refer to more than simply religious persuasion; they primarily mean attachment to one of two national cultural communities whose social intercommunication is kept to a minimum.

---

[18] Anthony Sampson, *The Essential Anatomy of Britain*, London 1992, pp. 151–53.

Large sections of the Catholic minority, whose national identity is different from that of the Protestant majority, demand that Northern Ireland should secede from the United Kingdom and join the Republic of Ireland in the south. The goal of the minority's nationalism is, not to gain autonomy, but to unite their homeland with an existing national state from which they have been forcibly separated.[19]

Common to all European regionalist movements is the way they stress the characteristics peculiar to a section of the population, and frequently draw attention to existing regional administrative and political institutions and traditions. Bringing historical, cultural and linguistic arguments to bear, they use their 'national' history, which is often steeped in myth, to legitimate political action. A collective identity emerges from consciousness of possessing a distinct historical tradition, culture and religion and of being embedded in specific social and economic forms of life.[20] This is all very familiar from the history of nineteenth-century Risorgimento nationalism. Like nationalism, regionalism also requires external forces to transform a usually apolitical feeling for one's home and region into a political movement. These might include a centralizing and standardizing state that denies a region traditional rights of self-government, or the impact of rapid social and economic modernization. General anxieties, resistance to life's increasing uniformity, localized xenophobia caused by immigration, protest against 'multinational' corporations replacing regionally based economic activity, and against historically evolved environments being destroyed by the march of progress: all these have been prominent elements of regionalism which, since the 1960s, has been supported by broad sections of society. Regionalists argue that one's geographical context must be graspable, that regional economies should be strengthened, and regional government be given more authority.

Some students of the subject, such as Michael Hechter, have interpreted regionalism as a reaction to 'internal colonialism'. This is a view supported by the rhetoric of regionalist movements themselves. The Corsicans, for instance, talk of Parisian cultural and economic colonization of their island, as do the Bretons undoubtedly. Growing awareness of social, economic and political underprivilege gives a decisive boost to regionalist tendencies. As Ernest Gellner has pointed out, uneven development of the economy disadvantages peripheral groups and may generate tensions between the centre and the margins of a country. Following Lenin and Antonio Gramsci, a number of American and British political scientists – Hechter, Gellner and Tom Nairn, for example – have drawn attention to this relationship.[21] They take England to be the fulcrum of political and economic power, with a Celtic periphery of Scotland, Wales and

---

[19] Sabine Wichert, *Northern Ireland since 1945*, London 1991. John Whyte, *Interpreting Northern Ireland*, Oxford 1990.

[20] Louis L. Snyder, *Global Mini-Nationalisms: Autonomy or Independence*, Westport (Conn.) 1982. Anthony D. Smith, *Nationalism in the Twentieth Century*, Oxford 1979, pp. 150–65.

[21] Michael Hechter, *Internal Colonialism. The Celtic Fringe in British National Development, 1536–1966*, London 1975. Ernest Gellner, *Thought and Change*, London 1964, pp. 147–78. Nairn, *Break-Up of Britain*.

Northern Ireland. Uneven economic development in the Celtic fringe and the prosperous parts of England, particularly in the 1980s, are not the chance outcome of more or less favourable local conditions, but of an unequal distribution of political power that allows some regions to expand at the expense of others. The result is a relationship of exploitation that amounts to 'internal colonialism'.

The thesis is unquestionably prone to exaggerate some aspects of the situation while failing adequately to mention others. Nevertheless, the United Kingdom does provide some evidence in its favour. As is well known, the Scottish and Welsh economies have suffered in recent years from declines in shipbuilding, the steel industry and coal mining. They are symptomatically often called 'depressed areas'. The Scots' sense of economic and social underprivilege *vis-à-vis* other parts of Britain combined with the hope that sensible use of North Sea oil would bring a new phase of prosperity to the Scottish economy; but it would seem that only Scottish institutions could use 'Scottish' oil to local advantage. The Scottish National Party's use of the North Sea oil reserves as a political issue is generally regarded as a great success.[22]

Regional economic differentiation as a generator of regionalism can also be fruitfully offered as a thesis to explain the situation in Catalonia and the Basque country. But here, neither of them have been economically ignored; indeed they form the heart of the Spanish economy. In these cases the regionalists argue they are denied self-determination precisely because of their economic power, and are hence exploited by 'Madrid'.[23]

Structural economic inequalities, uneven development within a state, and the inability – or reluctance – of politicians to iron them out, are no doubt important factors in the emergence of regionalism derived from economic grievances. But economic regionalism always goes hand in hand with local cultural and political aspirations. In each particular case, the combination of forces is different. The common bond between all varieties of regionalism, irrespective of their individual differences, is a firmly stated conviction that distinct and unitary social, historical, cultural and geographic groups exist, and that these must be given more say in running their local lives. It is a conviction that places them clearly in the tradition of nineteenth-century European national movements. Many regionalist organizations are aware of this, as their names suggest: Scottish National Party, Partido Nacionalista Vasco, Parti Nationaliste Occitan, Front de Libération Nationale de la Corse. For this reason Hugh Seton-Watson has described regionalism as unsatisfied nationalism; in other words, it has yet to create its own nation-state.[24] But the political aims of regionalism distinguish it from nationalism. Apart from the Basques and the more radical separatist wings in other countries, regionalist movements do not aspire to form their own national states. Usually their demands range from

---

[22] Robert Levy, *Scottish Nationalism at the Crossroads*, Edinburgh 1990.

[23] C. Abel and A. Torrents (eds), *Spain. Conditional Democracy*, London 1984.

[24] Hugh Seton-Watson, 'Unsatisfied Nationalism', in: *Journal of Contemporary History* 6 (1971), pp. 3–13.

cultural autonomy to the federalist restructuring of an existing state. In an extreme case, Corsican regionalists argue that their island community should share nothing but currency, foreign policy, defence and certain elements of the judicial system with mainland France.

The central governments in Madrid, Paris and London have reacted variously to the challenge they face from the regions. As the upholders of 'national unity' they have naturally dragged their heels. Post-Franco Spain, transformed into a federal kingdom in 1979 by a new democratic constitution, has been most accommodating of all to a problem that has a long history there. Since that date it has comprised 17 regions, each with its own government. The 'historic regions' of Catalonia, Euskadi (the Basque country), and Galicia, already self-governing before Franco took over, were the first to earn autonomy status, with Andalusia following.[25] The French government for its part initiated a cautious programme of decentralization that granted more responsibility to the regions. Regionalism was traditionally considered reactionary, however, and decentralization in France has not reached Spanish proportions, except with respect to Corsica. Since early 1982 the island has been the only French region to enjoy statutory autonomy, apparently in large measure a response to regionalist demands for a Corsican identity. In the summer of the same year, the Corsicans elected a representative body that has the right to set a modest budget.[26]

In the United Kingdom, regionalism has waned over the last few years. Devolution suffered a setback in 1979 when a referendum held in Wales and Scotland rejected the idea of decentralization. The plans originally tabled would have given both countries national representative bodies with administrative and, in Scotland, also legislative powers. But ultimately the delegation of responsibility away from London would not have reduced Westminster's sovereignty. As far as is known, there are no plans to change the governmental structure of Britain in this manner. In the general elections since 1979 Scottish and Welsh separatist parties have been only moderately successful, much to the disappointment of extremists with more far-reaching schemes (see Tables 5.1 and 5.2).

3 Nationalism after Communism in Eastern Europe

The sudden upsurge of seething ethnic nationalism in Eastern and South-Eastern Europe after the collapse of the communist regimes in the late 1980s and early 1990s took students of the subject almost completely by surprise. An ideology which communists attributed to bourgeois and capitalist society made an extraordinary comeback. Subsequent events in Eastern Europe, in the Soviet Union, in Yugoslavia and Czechoslovakia gave ample proof that nationalism's halcyon days are not yet drawing to a close. Once again, ethnically based Risorgimento nationalism turned out

---

[25] Abel and Torrents (eds), *Spain. Conditional Democracy.*
[26] Peter Savigear, 'Corsica', in: Michael Watson (ed.), *Contemporary Minority Nationalism*, London 1990, pp. 86–99.

to be a source of instability for the existing social and state order. Separatism, irredentism and expansionism founded on true or, more often, rather questionable historical claims, threatened established states, eventually caused their dissolution and triggered off ethnic wars. Social groups, nationalities and nations, among them some who had never possessed a state of their own in known history, demanded independence and their own nation-state. The number of states in Europe soared. At 43 in 1994, it had never been higher.

Nationalism, as in the decades after the French Revolution, once again manifested itself as a most powerful ideology – the destroyer and creator of states, the bearer of strong emotions and aspirations, the mover of feelings of solidarity, sacrifice and hatred. The quest for national autonomy, lost ethnic tradition and submerged cultural heritages triumphed over 'proletarian internationalism', communist brotherhood and the idea of the multinational polity. In those vast areas of Europe and Asia where communism once held unchallenged sway, subjected people were set free to decide for themselves, but freedom was accompanied by a frightening proliferation of bloody national conflicts, violence and 'national cleansing', a euphemism for persecution, deportation and genocide.[27]

The first communist state that had to surrender to the onslaught of nationalism was the Soviet Union where nationalism, according to the communist ideology, was supposed to have disappeared. In reality, however, the Soviet Union, once established, had suppressed those nationalist movements within it that were seeking independence. Instead, Moscow granted a sort of federal system ('union') with republics and autonomous regions along the lines of national identities. The clause in the Soviet constitution, however, that proclaimed the right of national self-determination remained a chimera right up to the very end of the union. The 'democratic centralism' of the Communist Party to which the republics and regions were subject meant that no real autonomy ever existed, let alone a right to secede from the Union.[28]

It was only in the mid-1980s that nationalist demands could be voiced in public. The decisive turning-point was Mikhail Gorbachev's rise to power as General Secretary of the Communist Party in March 1985. From that time on, demands for independence, accompanied by mass demonstrations and sometimes rioting, could be heard in peripheral regions of the Soviet Union, such as the Baltic republics, Armenia, Azerbaijan, Georgia, Kazakhstan, Uzbekistan and Moldavia near the Black Sea.[29] These were clearly manifestations of Risorgimento nationalism which splashed over into the Ukraine. The Russians themselves reacted with a kind of defensive nationalism which had very much in common with

---

[27] Misha Glenny, *Rebirth of History: Eastern Europe in the Age of Democracy*, Harmondsworth 1992.

[28] Bohdan Nahaylo, *Soviet Disunion. A History of the Nationalities Problem in the USSR*, London 1990. Gregory Gleason, *Federalism and Nationalism. The Struggle for Republican Rights in the USSR*, Boulder (Col.) 1990.

[29] Anthony Hyman, 'Moving out of Moscow's Orbit: The Outlook for Central Asia', in: *International Affairs* 69 (1993), pp. 289–304.

integral nationalism. Organizations such as *Pamyat* ('Memory') and *Interfront* were founded to safeguard Russian interests, the former including unmistakably anti-Semitic elements and the latter aiming to protect ethnic Russians in the non-Russian republics.[30] In Estonia, for example, Russians make up 40 per cent of the population, in Latvia 33 per cent, in the Ukraine 22 per cent, in Kazakhstan 38 per cent and Uzbekistan 11 per cent (1993).

The almost simultaneous upsurge of various forms of nationalism showed that under the iron fist of the authoritarian Soviet state a cauldron of suppressed nationalist aspirations and resentments had simmered for decades. Why they suddenly, and rather surprisingly for the outside world, burst into the open is a topic for speculation. But there are at least three factors which may help to explain the renaissance of nationalism in the twilight years of the Soviet empire. First, the gradual liberalization of the communist dictatorship under Gorbachev, which was encapsulated in the words *perestroika* ('reconstruction') and *glasnost* ('openness'), was the cause of unprecedented political mobilization. Gorbachev's programme included greater decentralization of the Union, especially in economic and budgetary matters. The weakening of the centralized police state permitted a hitherto unknown freedom to express dissident political views, and the watering-down of communist ideology created opportunities for political organizations to compete with the Communist Party. Changing political circumstances allowed nationalist political agitation where previously it was banned. They allowed the election of nationalist politicians or nationalist-supported governments in the republics (e.g., Lithuania and Estonia in the late 1980s). In December 1989, Lithuania was the first republic of the Soviet Union to form an independent Lithuanian Communist Party. In some cases Gorbachev himself appointed nationalistically inclined party leaders hoping to harness popular support for his modernizing reforms and the difficult rebuilding of the whole political system.

The prospect of reforms and the exhilarating experience of political, constitutional and economic change after decades of state authoritarianism necessarily had repercussions on the way people thought, which can be considered a second factor in the upsurge of nationalism and nationalist behaviour in the Soviet Union. When it thaws, expectations rise. Political reforms that expressly aimed at abolishing an inhuman regime, establishing liberal democracy and the rule of civil rights opened up a wide horizon. All of a sudden, everything seemed within reach. Hitherto suppressed nations and nationalities sensed their chance. A new 'springtime of the peoples' promised the fulfilment of dreams which only a few years earlier had seemed to be totally utopian. Consequently, nationalists became bolder and bolder.

Finally, a strong feeling of 'internal colonialism', continually fuelled by a long history of Russification in all parts of the Soviet Union, was a third factor in the nationalist take-off. Long-standing demands for the national

---

[30] James G. Kellas, *The Politics of Nationalism and Ethnicity*, Basingstoke 1991, p. 107. Alexander Bon/Robert van Voren (eds), *Nationalism in the USSR. Problems of Nationalities*, Amsterdam 1989, esp. pp. 28–43, 65–67, 87–95.

language to be made official were generally granted to the republics in 1989. The public display of national symbols such as the blue and yellow flag in the Ukraine was no longer banned. Economic dependence on a centralized and often inefficient bureaucracy in Moscow had long been a cause of resentment and feelings of discrimination. In Latvia, for example, Russians manned many factories which the Latvians saw as not primarily serving their own country but the needs and interest of the Soviet economy. Exploitation by centralized planning and forced industrialization without regard for the environment had to be replaced, in the opinion of the nationalists, by the development of truly national economies, which would use resources to their own benefit. Differential economic gains would no longer be tolerated.

In its initial phase the new Risorgimento nationalism in the multinational Soviet empire was a movement to break away from Russia, seen by the nations at the periphery as a colonial power. However, it was not always clear whether hitherto subjected nations and nationalities were seeking total independence or merely an improved autonomy in a more and truly federal Soviet Union. Once traditional fault-lines had gained a new meaning, national and religious boundaries had been recognized, many of the new republics on the territory of the former Soviet Union compromised, for various reasons, and remained constituent parts of the newly founded Commonwealth of Independent States (CIS).[31] The dominant partner in this commonwealth, which is rather loosely knit, is undoubtedly the Russian Federation, which had declared its own 'sovereignty' in June 1990. Russia in itself is a federation of 86 republics and regions as of 1992. Will dismemberment be its fate? It has yet to be seen to what extent the CIS and the Russian Federation will succeed in ending the seemingly continuous process of political secessions from larger political units. The result is already visible today: the balkanization of a vast area of the globe, which in modern times had come under the spell of one great empire.

The rule of the Tsars and their communist successors over Russia and its neighbouring countries had, after all, at least one advantage. It had pacified regions which, since the unleashing of nationalism at the end of the twentieth century, have become the victims of national conflicts and wars between new-born nations. These were and are conflicts not just between non-Russians and Russians. They are also wars between the nationalities themselves. A bloody struggle erupted in 1988, for example, between Armenians and Azeris over the region of Nagorno-Karabakh, an Armenian enclave in Azerbaijan. Other ethnic conflicts broke out in 1989 in Georgia between Abkhazis and Georgians, and in Moldavia between Moldavians, Ukrainians and Russians. A feature of all these conflicts is that the rise of one nationalism usually produces a reaction from others. At the end of the twentieth century, Europe, so it seems, is reliving its historical experiences of the nineteenth century: nationalism liberates

---

[31] Gail Lapidus *et al.* (eds), *From Union to Commonwealth. Nationalism and Separatism in the Soviet Republics*, Cambridge 1992.

individuals and nations but, at the same time, triggers off strife, hatred, bloodshed and endless misery. Once again, nationalism proves its power in politics and society at large. But at a cost: the distress and appalling suffering of individuals, young and old. They have been, and still are, victims of an ideology born in the turmoils of the French Revolution.

That nationalism brings with it indescribable suffering and destruction was also the experience of the peoples in former Yugoslavia. After the virtual downfall of communism, the Yugoslav federation broke up into its constituent republics which, with the possible exception of Slovenia in the north, were not ethnically homogeneous entities. During the 35 years of Marshal Tito's dictatorship (1945–80) Yugoslavia was governed as a unitary state. The republics and autonomous provinces (Vojvodina, Kosovo) were not more than executive organs of the political centre in Belgrade. Tito's dictatorial regime, the Communist Party, the civil and secret service, and the army were the clamps which held the state together. The decomposition of the state began after Tito's death in 1980. In a step-by-step process, fuelled by an over worsening economic crisis, power shifted from the centre to the republics. 'Yugoslavia' as a political idea had lost all attraction. The result, since 1989, has been independence for the republics, civil war, national expansionism and, accompanying it, widespread 'ethnic cleansing' on a scale not seen in Europe since the Second World War.[32]

Yugoslavia was an artificial product created at the end of the First World War and burdened right from its birth by the kinds of domestic troubles that had dominated the last decades of the Austro-Hungarian empire. Each of its nations claimed either a language, or a culture, or a religion and a specific historic memory. During the inter-war years, conflicts between nationalities, four religions (Catholic, Greek Orthodox, Islam and Protestantism), two scripts (Latin and Cyrillic) and several languages, had continually spawned new crises. Potentially, the country's very existence was always being questioned. Immediately after the Second World War, Yugoslav communists rather optimistically thought they had overcome the nationality related tensions that had always strained the Kingdom of the Serbs, Croats and Slovenes. Speaking on 'Nationalism and Internationalism' in late 1948, the communist leader Josip Broz Tito claimed that Yugoslavia had solved its national problems 'to the general satisfaction of all our peoples'.[33] Nationalism, by its very nature, remained anathema to the Yugoslav idea because such a state could only exist when nationalist thinking was kept at bay. This was quite different from the situation in Bulgaria or Romania where the communist dictators Todor Zhivkov and Nicolae Ceausescu very cleverly combined nationalism and Marxism-Leninism as the legitimizing twin pillars of their regimes' ideology.[34]

---

[32] Radovan Vukadinovic, *The Break-Up of Yugoslavia: Threats and Challenges*, The Hague 1992.

[33] Josip Broz Tito, *Sur le nationalisme et l'internationalisme*, Belgrade 1948, p. 7.

[34] Trond Gilberg, *Nationalism and Communism in Romania. The Rise and Fall of Ceausescu's Personal Dictatorship*, Boulder (Col.) 1990.

The foundations for the supra-national Yugoslav federation had been laid during the war of liberation against occupying Nazi forces, fought by the partisans under the motto of 'Brotherhood and Unity'. Even while the charismatic leader of Yugoslavia was still alive, however, it was not difficult to recognize that his statement of 1948 was more an idealized conception of the political situation than one based firmly on political reality. Tito was referring to a political programme that became the official doctrine of the communist state. Since then, any sense of community shared by all Yugoslavs has been no more than superficial, even though its intellectual roots can be traced back to mid-nineteenth century Yugoslavism, and the country's élite, particularly senior functionaries in the Communist Party, have actively promoted it.

In the wake of some cautious liberalization of the political system, evidence suggests that since the 1960s, socialist 'Yugoslavism' attaching to the country as a whole has been fading, while sectarian nationalisms among its peoples and nationalities (the term 'minority' was alien to official statements) had proved more durable, and possibly more powerful. The extremely complex ethnic mosaic to which Yugoslavia was home fuelled national clashes in which frequently forgotten historical tensions unexpectedly re-emerged to dominate the political stage. The intricacy of the pattern transformed some of the six constituent republics such as Macedonia, Serbia or Bosnia-Herzegovina into miniature multinational states. Another constant source of conflict was the delicate balance between administrative centralism from above and pressure for autonomy from below as well as the virtual dominance of the Serbs, who comprised more than 36 per cent of Yugoslavia's population (see Table 5.3). Other disruptive tensions between the various republics emanated from the traditional economic gap between northern and southern parts of the country.

Since the 1960s most support for national particularism had come from the lower echelons of the Communist Party in the constituent republics and from the regional intelligentsia. Though the arguments presented in each case were different, they were almost unanimous in the demand for a reform of state structures, which in detail meant decentralization, and parity status for Slovene and Macedonian with the Serbo-Croat language which was the *de facto* official language. The Slav Muslims, who made up a good 40 per cent of the population in Bosnia-Herzogovina, pointed to their religion and particular cultural traditions to underpin their demands for recognition as an independent nation in the Yugoslav state. This was granted in 1968, but failed to solve all their problems. In the autonomous province of Kosovo, which is part of Serbia, 77 per cent of the population are ethnic Albanians who in 1968 began demanding that their status be upgraded to that of a nation with its own constituent republic. Although their requests were almost completely satisfied in the 1970s, by the early 1980s the legal and political situation of the Albanian majority in Kosovo, one of the poorest parts of the country, was causing further unrest. The fact that Kosovo shares a common border with the independent Albanian nation-state made the situation even more difficult. In Albania irredentist rhetoric can always be easily whipped up.

Table 5.3 Ethnic groups in Yugoslavia (% of population in 1981)

Serbs	36.3	Albanians	7.7
Croats	19.7	Macedonians	6.0
Bosnian Muslims	8.9	Montenegrins	2.6
Slovenes	7.8	Hungarians	1.9

Consequently, Serbian nationalism was triggered off by the Kosovo problem. In 1986, more than two hundred Serbian intellectuals drafted a notorious memorandum for the Serbian parliament which drew attention to the allegedly desperate position of the Serbian minority in Kosovo. The petition claimed that these were the victims of expulsion and even genocide. Moreover, within Yugoslavia, Serbia was said always to have been disadvantaged. Its economic interests, so the memorandum maintained, had been continually subordinated to those of the industrially more developed republics of Slovenia and Croatia. At the heart of the matter there was undeniably uneven economic development in the various republics and provinces.[35]

Against this background of economic discontent and a weak collective Yugoslav presidency after Tito's death, nationalist rhetoric and propaganda made their predictable impact. In the following years the nationalist Slobodan Milosevic, a former communist, turned Serbia's feelings of discrimination and the alleged threat to its very existence into an aggressive policy of irredentism and expansionism. The policy of a 'Greater Serbia', which demanded the incorporation of Kosovo and other territories into Serbia, inevitably clashed with the political aspirations of the other republics. This speeded up the end of a state that had been widely regarded, particulary after 1945, as a successful experiment, demonstrating to the world that nationalism can be overcome and multinational states can prosper after all.

4 Nationalism in the Third World

Before the rather unexpected renaissance of nationalism in Eastern Europe, the former Soviet Union and Yugoslavia, the developing countries in Asia, Africa and Latin America were considered the hotbed of nationalism. For them nationalism had turned out to be a handy political ideology to mobilize the masses and socially integrate their newly founded states that were, in many cases, faced with huge problems of ethnic diversity, unstable political systems and disputed boundaries.

When the Second World War was over, the liberation of colonized peoples from European rule was inspired by the right of every nation to determine its own political destiny. The parallels with European Risorgimento nationalism are obvious. The intellectual and political leaders of

---

[35] See the article on Yugoslavia in: Margareta Mommsen (ed.), *Nationalismus in Osteuropa. Gefahrvolle Wege in die Demokratie*, Munich 1992, pp. 123–24.

the 'national liberation movements' in the colonies – men like Mahatma Gandhi, Ahmed Sukarno, Kwame Nkrumah, Léopold S. Senghor and Jomo Kenyatta – had mostly lived and been educated in Europe. They made no secret of the fact that they were using an ideology whose amazing power to change, to emancipate and to integrate peoples had been proved in Europe. In much the same way as liberal Risorgimento nationalism in Europe had been directed against existing structures of domination and the old multinational empires, nationalism in the Third World was now channelled against colonialism and the political, economic and cultural imperialism of the Europeans. It was to become the bond, if only temporarily, which held together a coalition of heterogeneous groups and organizations fighting the colonial powers and their indigenous collaborators. Whether it was at all possible to apply such basic concepts of European history as nation and nation-state to political conditions in the Third World was rarely the subject of debate.

It took far less time for the peoples of colonized regions to win their independence than had been generally expected in Europe as well as in the colonies themselves. The Cold War between East and West and the anticolonial stance of the United States certainly helped. The colonized people used negotiation or armed struggle (or both) to free themselves and, in terms of international law, to establish sovereignty in 'nation-states'. But although social and political emancipation for the individual had been promised as part and parcel of the liberation of the people from colonial domination, things often turned out different in reality. Pledges of political and social freedom in the young states were reserved for occasional appearance in political manifestos. On the whole, the liberal components so central to European Risorgimento nationalism were assigned no more than marginal significance by its non-European counterpart. Yet in neither case did nationalist ideology become obsolete once independence was declared. All the evidence suggests that non-European nationalism, which the American historian Louis Snyder has called 'new nationalism', continues to perform important functions.[36]

Despite all the similarities of appearance and rhetoric they share with European Risorgimento nationalism, we must constantly bear in mind that the circumstances surrounding Third World national movements were fundamentally different. They emerged in areas where cultural, ethnic and linguistic homogeneity was the exception rather than the rule, and where the population lived in political units designed by European colonial administrations. This was true of India, Indonesia, Sri Lanka, Nigeria, Cameroon and Zimbabwe, to name only a few examples. Here independence meant the end of state-building; but it ushered in a new phase of arduous and prolonged nation-building. In order to satisfy the central postulate of the nation-state, the task now at hand was to turn a population frequently characterized by enormous differences of language, religion and ethnicity into a national unit. The few unifying bonds operative in these new states, now all referred to as 'developing countries' in terms

---

[36] Louis L. Snyder, *The New Nationalism*, Ithaca (NY) 1968.

of their economic as well as their political systems, were related almost exclusively to the experience of colonial rule and the will to throw out the foreign regime. Clearly, the further memories of colonial oppression and social discrimination by a foreign élite slipped into the past, the more the reserve of common experience and solidarity threatened to dry up.[37]

In this situation, nation-building became crucial for maintaining the precarious stability of the new states. Anticolonial nationalism had hitherto been dominated by negative aims, the destruction of the colonial regime foremost among them; these now had to be turned into positive ones conducive to the new state's political and social integration and the creation of a coherent nation. Ethnicity, history and culture could only rarely, however, form the bases of the 'nation' in the Third World as they had done for the European cultural nation; the fundamental parameters here are, rather, the territory of the state that emerged from decolonization, a system of mores and norms, and an image of society and the world that, according to nationalist propaganda, is deemed unique to the inhabitants. Key terms were, for instance, 'African socialism', *'ujamaa'* ('public spirit' or 'family spirit'), *'négritude'*, 'new order', and 'African humanism', distinguishing the nationalism of one state from that of others. The concept of the political nation was supplemented by specific additions.

In many cases, the political leaders of the new countries turned to pre-colonial history to lend legitimacy to their 'nations'. They gave them the names of polities that used to exist on the same soil in the past – Ghana, Sri Lanka, Myanmar, Benin, Zaire, Zimbabwe, Burkina Faso – and looked to real or putative traditions in choosing their official symbols. The Indian coat of arms shows one of the lion capitals at the holy place of Sarnath in Uttar Pradesh, where Buddha first preached after his enlightenment. Another example is the Algerian flag: green is the colour of the prophet, red of socialism, white of purity; the crescent-moon with the star is the symbol of Islam. The history of Risorgimento nationalism demonstrates that similar efforts were also made in Europe from the nineteenth century onwards to legitimate nation and state by history, and reinforce national consciousness by drawing upon a culture which was claimed to be indigenous.

In short, leading politicians in most of the new states after 1945 have harnessed nationalism in an attempt to turn a rather mixed people living in a state into a political nation. Individuals were encouraged to show allegiance to the state's 'nation' of which they have become a member irrespective of their religious, cultural, tribal or ethnic ties. In order to obviate the practically inevitable conflicts over language and the associated political clashes, most of the new states in the Third World opted against awarding any indigenous ethnic tongue the status of official language. Pakistan tried it with Urdu, and the assimilatory language policy pursued by the central government only strengthened the desire in Bengali-speaking East Pakistan for secession. In almost all former British

---

[37] See the chapters by Hugh Tinker and Arnold Hughes in: Leonard J. Tivey (ed.), *The Nation-State. The Formation of Modern Politics*, Oxford 1981.

colonies, English thus continues to be the official language, and often the vernacular; likewise, French is still spoken in former French colonies. The language of the former colonial power serves as the *lingua franca* in government and economy.[38]

The role nationalism currently plays in Third World countries is thus to consolidate the state and sustain the process of nation-building. National ideology serves to integrate heterogeneous social, religious and ethnic groups, and to segregate them from groups beyond the state's borders, even though they rarely share national characteristics in the conventional sense of the term. The problem is that in many cases alternative modes of integration are not an option. Consequently, in the new states nationalism is presented as a progressive and constructive force, a consciousness-raising medium for collective self-discovery following the often traumatic experience of colonial oppression and enforced westernization. Nationalism defines a way of overcoming sectional interests in the post-colonial state and arriving at a new social order. The Kenyan political scientist Ali Mazrui, who mainly lives in the United States, neatly summed up the situation when he said that in Africa nationalism is searching for a Utopia that knows no tribes,[39] for these are the political units most reluctant to accept nation-building by the central governments. Tribalism and nationalism are opposites.[40]

Beneath the surface, however, it frequently transpires that nationalism in the Third World very often is a political strategy serving to divert attention away from unresolved domestic problems and incomplete social integration. In many cases, the same can be said of Europe past and present. Nationalism then takes the form of rhetorical aggression against neighbouring countries supposedly presenting a threat or occupying territory felt to belong to the nation. Directed towards the outside world, nationalism lays claim to lands, and will go as far as armed conflict in order to satisfy its aspirations. There are signs that in the Third World, too, nationalism will be transformed from an ideology of liberation and emancipation to one of diversion.

Latin America, in particular, provides much evidence to show how nationalism is manipulated to defuse domestic tension. Since independent states began to emerge in the early nineteenth century from the *audiencias* – the judicial and administrative regions – of the Spanish Empire, nationalism in the Latin American republics has had as coloured a history as it did in Europe.[41] Given expression in the nineteenth century by

---

[38] H. S. Wilson, *African Decolonization*, London 1993. W. H. Morris-Jones/Georges Fischer (eds), *Decolonization and After. The British and French Experience*, London 1980, esp. Chapter III 'Institutions and Cultures', pp. 241–345.

[39] Ali A. Mazrui, 'Africa: The Political Culture of Nationhood and the Political Economy of the State', in: *Millennium. Journal of International Studies* 12 (1983), p. 210. See also B. Neuberger, 'The Western Nation-State in African Perceptions of Nation-Building', in: *Asian and African Studies* 11 (1976), pp. 241–61, and idem, 'State and Nation in African Thought', in: *Journal of African Studies* 4 (1977), pp. 198–205.

[40] W. J. Argyle, 'European Nationalism and African Tribalism', in: P. H. Gulliver (ed.), *Tradition and Transition in East Africa*, London 1969, pp. 41–57.

[41] John Lynch, *The Spanish-American Revolutions, 1808–1826*, New York 1973.

landowners and the upper-middle classes, it functioned mainly to further nation-building and to legitimate the rule of the Creole élite. It drew a veil over class conflicts and social tension, and concealed the fact that no attempt was made to reform the colonial economic and social system in a way that would have brought about the political and social liberation of the masses.

Then in the twentieth century, nationalism in Latin America underwent a profound change. Intellectuals from the slowly emergent middle class traced underdevelopment and the lack of social justice they perceived around them back to imbalances in the relations between their countries and the industrialized nations, especially the United States. Nationalism shifted to become increasingly a counterweight to existing economic, cultural and political dependence. Mexico in particular stepped to the fore, embarking on a new phase of national integration after the revolution in 1910. Since then, the endeavours by Mexico and other countries of the American continent to end underdevelopment and dependency have been accompanied by an often passionate rejection of North America's hegemonial claims in the 'western hemisphere' and of the power of foreign big business.[42] In other words, Latin American nationalism today is directed both to the inside and the outside; it parries United States' influence and highlights the dependency and domestic conflicts that had been more or less submerged by national rhetoric following independence. The intellectuals who give expression to it are mainly middle class, though the working class and army officers are also represented; they perceive nationalism as a powerful instrument to throw off external bondage and engender political and social freedom at home.[43]

How successful, then, has nationalism in the Third World been as an ideology of political and social integration? The question can only be answered by examining precisely what has happened in each country since independence. Even a general answer that overlooks essential differences between the various states can only be provisional. Indeed, it is perhaps too early to pose the question. Nevertheless, if one looks at the history of the new states in Africa and Asia since achieving independence after the Second World War, it is striking that their frontiers, which in most cases were arbitrarily drawn, have hitherto proved to be surprisingly stable. Very few borders have been re-routed, and political secession has remained the exception. This is astonishing in view of the enormous problems of integration, the powerful internal tensions and the many potential social fractures that developing countries in the Third World face.

Desires to change territorial shapes or to force secessions are of course not entirely unknown. In 1963, for instance, the rich mining province of Shaba (formerly Katanga) tried unsuccessfully to break away from Zaire. With the tacit support of all other African states, in 1967–70 the central

---

[42] R. F. Smith, *The United States and Revolutionary Nationalism in Mexico 1916–1932*, Chicago 1972. V. Alba, *The Mexicans. The Making of a Nation*, New York 1967.

[43] Gerhard Masur, *Nationalism in Latin America. Diversity and Unity*, London 1966. L. L. Snyder, 'Populist Nationalism in Latin America', in: *idem*, *The New Nationalism*, Ithaca (NY) 1968, pp. 217–48.

government of Nigeria used its military power to foil the attempts of the Ibo people of Biafra, in the south-eastern part of the country, to secede.[44] The attitude of Africa's leaders in this case was governed by the fear that if oil-rich Biafra successfully broke away from Nigeria, similar attempts in other regions throughout the continent might follow. The Organization of African Unity (OAU) subsequently denied the right to secession, and is thus guaranteeing current territorial arrangements. In the rest of the developing world, Bangladesh remains the only country to have gone its own way. Its secession from Pakistan in 1971 was helped by two factors: geography – Bangladesh (East Pakistan) is separated from West Pakistan by some 1,000 miles of Indian territory; and the active support of a neighbouring state – India backed East Pakistani leaders when they began to work for separation from West Pakistan, and in the end provided military aid.

The stability of post-colonial borders (which have also been maintained because the new states insisted the United Nations do so) says nothing at all, however, about the success of nation-building in the Third World. It is a process not far advanced in most cases, and therefore unrest and conflict continually come to the surface in these parts of the world. Countries such as India, Sri Lanka, Iraq, Chad, Nigeria, Sudan and Cameroon are all products of colonialism; they are conglomerates of numerous peoples and tribes, linguistic and religious minorities. By comparison, the nationality problems that brought down Europe's old multinational empires at the end of the First World War appear mere trivia. It is clear that these states can only temporarily manage to contain tensions that exist between their various constituent groups. Almost fifty years after the subcontinent was released from British colonial rule, the central government in India, for example, is burdened by the desire of states such as Assam and Nagaland and religious minorities such as the Sikhs to secede from the republic. Whether India is a multilingual nation or a multinational state is still open to debate. The only conclusion the history of twentieth-century Southern Asia prompts is that nationalism has been an effective weapon for liberation from colonial rule; but in most cases has been powerless to build and sustain a solid political order.

Sri Lanka, politically united again under British rule after having been divided into small kingdoms for centuries, is threatened by civil war between the Buddhist Sinhalese and the Tamil minority of around one-fifth of the population. Sinhalese nationalism produced reactive Tamil nationalism whose aim is a separate Tamil state ('Eelam'). In Nigeria, and elsewhere, 'tribalism', which to African ears is a largely pejorative term for the desire for autonomy, is a major obstacle to nation-building. As in many parts of the developing world, the Nigerian military regards itself as the nation's protector and the guardian of national unity and dignity. As far as the movements pressing for autonomy are concerned, their state's nationalism is artificial and harks back to colonial days. 'Tribalism' is by

---

[44] James G. Kellas, *The Politics of Nationalism and Ethnicity*, Basingstoke 1991, pp. 124–25.

contrast based on natural identities that have survived the colonial era.[45] Many historians of post-colonial Africa have also adopted this argument by interpreting 'tribalism' as an element of anti-colonial African nationalism and as evidence of original national movements. For the time being, the problems are enormous. The Sudan, for instance, is unable to bridge the yawning gap between the Islamic, Arab north, with Khartoum as the capital, and the south whose population is a mixture of ethnic and religious groups. In Cameroon, that 'Africa in miniature', a single party, a centralized trade-union movement and a one-party state are faced with the task of creating a nation from some 200 tribes, 124 languages and dialects and four different religions.

The histories of Cameroon, Nigeria and other new states in the Third World suggests that nation-building programmes have often suffered severe setbacks because the ruling élites, to some extent pursuing a policy of 'tribalism' from above, seek the support of a particular ethnic or religious group, who, they hope, will help maintain and strengthen their rule in exchange for privilege. Such strategies, however, tend to produce just the opposite effect, by bringing to a head existing tensions within the 'nation', and thus clearing the way for militant, secessionist 'liberation movements' now launched, not against a European colonial power, but against the independent state that emerged from colonialism. As a result, these second-generation 'liberation movements' obviously violate a sacrosanct principle of contemporary international law. But then who is entitled to political self-determination? This has been a moot point since 1945. The majority of the United Nations member states seem to reserve the right only for certain peoples and ethnic minorities. In so doing they have tangibly narrowed down the concept of self-determination, lending it validity only with respect to those groups seeking an end to colonial dependence on European powers, and thus practically ruling out all other possible circumstances.

Apart from nationalism, separatism and 'tribalism', there have been no other significant challenges to nation-state arrangements in the Third World, nor to the dominance of the nation-state as a conceptual category. The situation in Europe from the nineteenth century onwards was not greatly different. In the developing world, nation-building has been given priority because national identities have either been entirely lacking or only very weak. Pan-Africanism essentially ceased to be a political force once decolonization was under way, and politicians such as Kwame Nkrumah, Jomo Kenyatta, Julius Nyerere, Hastings Banda, Léopold S. Senghor and Sékou Touré tried to combat the impending 'balkanization' of the African continent. Under the slogan, 'We are all Africans', they claimed the existence of an African identity powerful enough even to override the great differences between 'British' and 'French' Africa, between Africa north and south of the Sahara.

---

[45] John Breuilly, *Nationalism and the State*, Manchester 1982, p. 167. W. J. Argyle, 'European Nationalism and African Tribalism', in: P. H. Gulliver (ed.), *Tradition and Transition in East Africa*, London 1969, pp. 41–57.

African political and economic unity was originally the idea of Afro-Americans.[46] Their day came in 1963 when the Organization of African Unity (OAU) was founded in Addis Ababa. By comparison with the more ambitious plans occasionally tabled by Kwame Nkrumah, then undisputed ruler of Ghana, the OAU was an unsatisfactory compromise. As a kind of alliance for peace, good relations between African states are its main concern, its charter requiring members to respect the territorial integrity of other states and not to intervene in their internal affairs. The charter urges them to settle their differences peaceably, but does not explicitly oblige them to go to one another's aid in cases of external aggression. Quite obviously, member states are aware of the specific 'national' problems they face, and hope to maintain the status quo by taking the wind out of the sails of any irredentist tendencies from the very outset. The OAU provides a discussion forum for politicians from African states. Its real value lies in its ability to mediate and conciliate when conflict arises between member countries.

Pan-Arabism has also failed to make headway, both in practical and ideological terms, against the nationalisms of individual Arab countries from the Atlantic to the Persian Gulf, even though they probably form the most homogeneous cultural unit in the entire Third World. Following Gamal Abdel Nasser's death in 1970, the idea that Egypt could unite the Arab nations around it, as Piedmont and Prussia had once done in Europe, lost credibility and drive. For a long time the major force for cementing Arab solidarity was the Palestinian problem, and particularly their common rejection of Israel, which overshadowed all their other political and ideological differences. The cracks that have appeared in this united anti-Israeli front, however, have weakened the binding power of Pan-Arabism, which generally suffers the stigma of being only a veil for hegemonial ambitions of one or other of the Arab states.[47] One indication of this is the declining influence of the Arab League, an organization which since 1945 has obliged Arab countries to co-ordinate their foreign policies and to resolve their own rivalries peacefully. Pan-Arabism's weakness is further evidenced by the fact that the Arab states of North Africa have simultaneously belonged to both the OAU and the Arab League, yet have hitherto easily managed to avoid serious problems in the foreign-policy sphere.

Although we must recognize the inability of Pan-movements to place any significant brake on the march of nationalism since the nineteenth century, attempts are constantly being made to ease and to intensify co-operation across national boundaries. This political energy suggests that a rearrangement of the world order is possible. It would be an order in which nationally oriented thought and action are increasingly giving way to supra-national joint efforts at the regional level. The Arab League, the

---

[46] Imanuel Geiss, *The Pan-African Movement*, London 1974, p. 11. J. Ayodele Langley, *Pan-Africanism and Nationalism in West Africa 1900–1945*, Oxford 1973 (reprint 1978), pp. 17–23.

[47] Barry Rubin, 'Pan-Arab Nationalism: The Ideological Dream as Compelling Force', in: Jehuda Reinharz/George L. Mosse (eds), *The Impact of Western Nationalisms*, London 1992, pp. 181–98.

European Union, the Organization of African Unity, the Association of Southeast Asian Nations (ASEAN, formed in 1967), the Andean Pact (1969), and the Organization of Eastern Caribbean States (1981) are all examples of such attempts. They appear to be the foundation stones of a world order whose shape will become much clearer in the future, an order in which nationalism and the nation-state principle will have forfeited their absolute validity. This will be true not only of relations between states but also within those states, as federalism increasingly begins to take the place of centralism, not only in Europe and North America, as a means of organizing large political entities.

5 The Poverty of Nationalism

Nationalism, to all intents and purposes, means undisguised political egoism. As an ideology it preaches solidarity with and willingness to make sacrifices to one particular social group which, since the French Revolution of 1789, has been called the nation. Nationalism is rather exclusive in its dedication to the elevated nation and only too ready to ignore the interests of other groups, be it within the nation or a neighbouring nation. Intellectually, therefore, nationalism is clearly an extremely poor ideology and no match whatsoever for the great bodies of thought that constitute socialism or liberalism, the two other great ideologies originating in the late eighteenth and nineteenth centuries. The intellectual poverty of nationalism is amply mirrored by the fact that there are virtually no nationalist thinkers of any relevance. Herder and Mazzini come perhaps closest to being considered founding-fathers of the ideology of nationalism. Herder, however, was a philosopher with a much broader spectrum of ideas among which nationalism was only of secondary importance. And Mazzini's nationalist writing is rather dull and far from being of any inspirational value to national movements elsewhere. In short, nationalism lacks both fundamental or classic texts and original thinkers, which would have been the basis for a whole edifice of thought. Instead, nationalism boils down to two or three somewhat simplistic statements, of dubious general validity, on the pre-eminence of an 'imagined community'.[48]

Yet, despite all its obvious intellectual limitations and shortcomings, nationalism has proved to be an enormously powerful ideology over the last two centuries. There is no reason to assume that its astonishing grip on the masses all over the world will weaken in the decades ahead. One may even suggest that its conspicuous simplicity was, is and will be an essential feature of its amazing role in the history of humankind in the past, present and future. In times of political and social oppression, of profound changes in society and economic crises, nationalism seems to become irresistible to individuals and groups alike as a shelter and refuge from the challenges of life. For Europeans in the nineteenth century,

---

[48] Benedict Anderson, *Imagined Communities. Reflections on the Origin and Spread of Nationalism*, 3rd ed., London 1986.

nationalism beckoned, offering hope and liberation from unwanted political domination, and so it did for colonized peoples overseas after the Second World War and, once again, for East Europeans in the twilight of communism at the end of the 1980s. Nationalism's intensity may periodically fluctuate, but recent history offers only few perspectives for a world free of nationalist madness. One hope is that the newly founded or liberated nation-states of Eastern Europe are apparently prepared to see their independence as an achievement of long-held national aspirations, but at the same time only as a stepping-stone on their path towards an integrating Europe, firmly founded on liberal democracy, tolerance and protection of minorities.

In the closing years of the twentieth century nationalism has, for many contemporaries, almost completely lost its former liberal appeal, its credibility as the creator of a potentially better and more peaceful world of prosperous nation-states, and its vision of equality and justice everywhere and for everyone. In the twentieth century nationalism has shamelessly revealed its brutal face, its destructive powers in society and international relations, its constant threat to civilization and humanity. Events in former Yugoslavia and the Caucasus are once again the writing on the wall, a portent of things to come. What Lord Acton prophesied as early as 1862, in the heyday of liberal Risorgimento nationalism, has become the daily experience of today: 'Nationality [= nationalism] does not aim either at liberty or prosperity, both of which it sacrifices to the imperative necessity of making the nation the mould and measure of the State. Its course will be marked with material as well as moral ruin, in order that a new invention may prevail over the works of God and the interests of mankind.'[49]

At the dawn of a new millennium nationalism, the 'new invention', is far from being a spent force. It may have lost its former fervour in places such as Western Europe. But even there the question might rightly be asked whether a 'European nationalism' is not now looming on the horizon. Seen from Asia or Africa a policy of 'fortress Europe' can look like nationalism, but in a new guise. In much the same way Islamic fundamentalism in countries such as Algeria, Egypt, Sudan or Iran may also be interpreted as a new form of nationalism. Both examples will only confirm historical experience that nationalism is a kind of chameleon which adapts its colours to changing situations just as it likes. We can thus only conclude that nationalism is a constant danger to modern society, either real or latent, and an antidote has yet to be found. At present it is essential to accept the facts, however depressing they may be. Nevertheless, there is an urgent need to keep explaining the underlying causes of nationalism and its functions in the modern world, in an attempt to contain its appalling impact on individuals and society at large, and to counteract its primitive message of prejudice, intolerance and hatred. Success in this, however limited, may help humankind to survive in the twenty-first century.

---

[49] John E. Acton, 'Nationality', in: *idem, Essays on Freedom and Power*, ed. by Gertrude Himmelfarb, London 1956, p. 169.

Select Bibliography

I General and Comparative Studies

Anderson, B., *Imagined Communities. Reflections on the Origin and Spread of Nationalism*, 3rd ed., London 1986.

Baron, S. W., *Modern Nationalism and Religion*, New York 1960.

Berlin I., 'Nationalism. Past Neglect and Present Power', in: *idem, Against the Current. Essays in the History of Ideas*, London 1979, pp. 333–55.

Birch, A. H., *Nationalism and National Integration*, London 1989.

Boucher, J. *et al.* (eds), *Ethnic Conflict. International Perspectives*, Newbury Park (Calif.) 1987.

Breuilly, J., *Nationalism and the State*, Manchester 1982.

Carr, E. H., *Nationalism and After*, 2nd ed. London 1967.

Deutsch, K. W., *Nationalism and Social Communication. An Inquiry into the Foundations of Nationality*, 2nd ed., Cambridge (Mass.) 1966.

—— and W. J. Foltz (eds), *Nation-Building*, 2nd ed., New York 1966.

Doob, L., *Patriotism and Nationalism: Their Psychological Foundations*, New Haven (Conn.) 1964.

Featherstone, M. (ed.), *Global Culture: Nationalism, Globalisation and Modernity*, London 1990.

Gellner, E., *Thought and Change*, 3rd ed., London 1972.

—— *Nations and Nationalism*, Oxford 1983.

Greenfeld, L., *Nationalism. Five Roads to Modernity*, Cambridge (Mass.) 1992.

Hayes, C. J. H., *Essays on Nationalism* (1926), repr. New York 1966.

—— *Nationalism. A Religion*, New York 1960.

—— *The Historical Evolution of Modern Nationalism* (1931), repr. New York 1963.

Hobsbawm, E. J., 'Some Reflections on Nationalism', in: T. J. Nossiter *et al.* (eds), *Imagination and Precision in the Social Sciences. Essays in Memory of Peter Nettl*, Atlantic Heights (NJ) 1972, pp. 385–406.

—— *Nations and Nationalism since 1780. Programme, Myth, Reality*, Cambridge 1990.

Huizinga, J., 'Patriotism and Nationalism in European History', in: *idem, Men and Ideas. Essays on History, the Middle Ages, the Renaissance*, New York 1959, pp. 97–155.

Johnson, H. G. (ed.), *Economic Nationalism in Old and New States*, London 1968.

Kamenka, E. (ed.), *Nationalism. The Nature and Evolution of an Idea*, London 1976.

Kedourie, E., *Nationalism*, 3rd ed., London 1966.

Kellas, J. G., *The Politics of Nationalism and Ethnicity*, Basingstoke 1991.

Kemiläinen, A., *Nationalism. Problems Concerning the Word, the Concept, and Classification*, Jyvaskyla 1964.
Kohn, H., *The Age of Nationalism* (1962), repr. Westport (Conn.) 1976.
Mayall, J., *Nationalism and International Society*, Cambridge 1990.
Minogue, K. R., *Nationalism*, London 1967.
Michener, R. (ed.) *Nationality, Patriotism and Nationalism in Liberal Democratic Societies*, St. Paul (Minn.) 1993.
Mitchison, R. (ed.), *The Roots of Nationalism. Studies in Northern Europe*, Edinburgh 1980.
Nationalism. A Report by a Study Group of Members of the Royal Institute of International Affairs (1939), repr. New York 1965.
Palumbo, M. and W. O. Shanahan (eds), *Nationalism: Essays in Honor of Louis L. Snyder*, Westport (Conn.) 1981.
Schulze, H. (ed.), *Nation-Building in Central Europe*, Leamington Spa 1987.
Seton-Watson, H., *Nationalism, Old and New*, Sydney 1965.
—— *Nations and States. An Enquiry into the Origins of Nations and the Politics of Nationalism*, London 1977.
Shafer, B. C., *Nationalism. Interpreters and Interpretations*, 2nd ed., Washington 1963.
—— *Faces of Nationalism. New Realities and Old Myths*, New York 1972.
—— *Nationalism and Internationalism. Belonging in Human Experience*, Malabar (Flor.) 1982.
—— 'Debated Problems in the Study of Nationalism', in: *Canadian Review of Studies in Nationalism* 11 (1984), pp. 1–19.
Smith, A. D., *Nationalism in the Twentieth Century*, Oxford 1979.
—— *Theories of Nationalism*, 2nd ed., London 1983.
—— *The Ethnic Origins of Nations*, Oxford 1986.
—— (ed.), *Nationalist Movements*, London 1976.
Snyder, L. L., *The Meaning of Nationalism*, New York 1954.
—— *Varieties of Nationalism. A Comparative Study*, Hinsdale (Ill.) 1976.
Talmon, J. L., *The Myth of the Nation and the Vision of Revolution. The Origins of Ideological Polarisation in the Twentieth Century*, London 1981.

II Towards a Typology of Nationalism

Ahmad, F., *The Making of Modern Turkey*, London 1993.
Almog, S., *Nationalism and Antisemitism in Modern Europe*, Oxford 1990.
Anderson, P. R., *The Background of Anti-English Feeling in Germany 1890–1902*, 2nd ed., New York 1969.
Ashkenasi, A., *Modern German Nationalism*, New York 1976.
Beasley, W. G., *The Meiji Restoration*, Stanford (Calif.) 1973.
Bellamy, R., 'Liberalism and Nationalism in the Thought of Max Weber', in: *History of European Ideas* 14 (1992), pp. 499–507.
Berdahl, R. M., 'New Thoughts on German Nationalism', in: *American Historical Review* 77 (1972), pp. 65–80.
Berghahn, V. R., *Modern Germany. Society, Economy and Politics in the Twentieth Century*, Cambridge 1982.
Braddock, J., *The Greek Phoenix*, London 1972.
Carr, W., *A History of Germany 1815–1990*, 4th ed., London 1991.
Carsten, F. L., *The Rise of Fascism*, 2nd ed., London 1982.
Chickering, R., *We Men Who Feel Most German. A Cultural Study of the Pan-German League, 1886–1914*, London 1984.

Clogg, R. (ed.), *The Struggle for Greek Independence. Essays to Mark the 150th Anniversary of the Greek War of Independence*, Hamden (Conn.) 1973.

Colls, R. and P. Dodd (eds), *Englishness. Politics and Culture 1880–1920*, London 1986.

Craig, G. A., *Germany 1866–1945*, Oxford 1978.

Craig, J. E., *Scholarship and Nation Building. The Universities of Strasbourg and Alsatian Society 1870–1939*, Chicago 1984.

Dakin, D., *The Greek Struggle for Independence 1821–1833*, London 1973.

Dann, O. and J. Dinwiddy (eds), *Nationalism in the Age of the French Revolution*, London 1988.

De Grand, A. J., *The Italian Nationalist Association and the Rise of Fascism in Italy*, London 1978.

Deringil, S., 'The Ottoman Origins of Kemalist Nationalism: Namik Kemal to Mustafa Kemal', in: *European History Quarterly* 23 (1993), pp. 165–91.

Eisenstadt, S. N. and S. Rokkan (eds), *Building States and Nations. Models and Data Resources*, 2 vols, Beverly Hills (Calif.) 1973.

Eley, G., *Reshaping the German Right. Radical Nationalism and Political Change after Bismarck*, New Haven (Conn.) 1980.

Fishman, J. A., *Language and Nationalism. Two Integrative Essays*, Rowley (Mass.) 1973.

Gourvish, T. R. and A. O'Day (eds), *Later Victorian Britain, 1867–1900*, Basingstoke 1988.

Grainger, J. H., *Patriotisms. Britain 1900–1939*, London 1986.

Hales, E. E. Y., *Mazzini and the Secret Societies. The Making of a Myth*, London 1956.

Herzfeld, M., *Ours Once More: Folklore, Ideology and the Making of Modern Greece*, Austin 1982.

Heyd, U., *Foundations of Turkish Nationalism*, Westport (Conn.) 1979.

Hildebrand, K., *The Third Reich*, 3rd ed., London 1985.

Hirschfeld, G., *Nazi Rule and Dutch Collaboration. The Netherlands under German Occupation 1940–1945*, Oxford 1988.

Holton, D. C., *Modern Japan and Shinto Nationalism*, Chicago 1943.

Hoover, A. L., *The Gospel of Nationalism. German Patriotic Preaching from Napoleon to Versailles*, Stuttgart 1986.

Hughes, M., *Nationalism and Society. Germany 1800–1945*, London 1988.

Jarausch, K. H., *Students, Society, and Politics in Imperial Germany. The Rise of Academic Illiberalism*, Princeton (NJ) 1982.

Jenkins, B., *Nationalism in France. Class and Nation since 1789*, London 1990.

Kennedy, P. and A. J. Nicholls (eds), *Nationalist and Racialist Movements in Britain and Germany before 1914*, London 1981.

Kershaw, I., *The Nazi Dictatorship. Problems and Perspectives of Interpretation*, London 1985.

—— *The 'Hitler Myth'. Image and Reality in the Third Reich*, Oxford 1987.

Kinross, J., *Atatürk. The Rebirth of a Nation*, London 1964.

Kohn, H., *American Nationalism. An Interpretative Essay*, New York 1957.

—— *The Mind of Germany. The Education of a Nation*, London 1965.

Kolb, E., *The Weimar Republic*, London 1988.

Kushner, D., *The Rise of Turkish Nationalism, 1876–1908*, London 1977.

Lewis, B., *The Emergence of Modern Turkey*, 2nd ed., Oxford 1969.

Lipset, S. M., *The First New Nation. The United States in Historical and Comparative Perspective*, New York 1963.

McDowall, D., *The Kurds: A Nation Divided*, London 1992.

Merritt, R. L., *Symbols of American Community, 1735–1775*, New Haven (Conn.) 1966.

Mosse, G. L., *The Nationalization of the Masses. Political Symbolism and Mass Movements in Germany from the Napoleonic Wars through the Third Reich*, New York 1975.
—— *The Crisis of German Ideology. Intellectual Origins of the Third Reich*, New York 1981.
—— (ed.), *International Fascism. New Thoughts and New Approaches*, London 1979.
Newman, G., *The Rise of English Nationalism. A Cultural History 1740–1830*, London 1987.
Nolte, E., *Three Faces of Fascism. Action Française, Italian Fascism, National Socialism*, New York 1965.
Pflanze, O., 'Nationalism in Europe, 1848–1871', in: *Review of Politics* 28 (1966), pp. 129–43.
Rogger, H. and E. Webber (eds), *The European Right. A Historical Profile*, Berkeley (Calif.) 1965.
Rutkoff, P. M., *Revanche and Revision. The Ligue des Patriotes and the Origins of the Radical Right in France, 1882–1900*, Athens (Ohio) 1981.
Saint Clair, W., . . . *That Greece Might Still Be Free. The Philhellenes in the War of Independence*, London 1972.
Scott, I., *The Rise of the Italian State. A Study of Italian Politics during the Period of Unification*, Meerut 1980.
Seton-Watson, C., *Italy from Liberalism to Fascism 1870–1925*, London 1967.
Shaw, S. J., *History of the Ottoman Empire and Modern Turkey*, 2 vols, Cambridge 1977/78.
Shevin Coetzee, M., *The German Army League. Popular Nationalism in Wilhelmine Germany*, Oxford 1990.
Smiley, D., *The Canadian Political Nationality*, Toronto 1967.
Smith, A., *The Emergence of a Nation State. The Commonwealth of England 1529–1660*, London 1984.
Smith, W. D., *The Ideological Origins of Nazi Imperialism*, New York 1986.
Snyder, L. L., *Roots of German Nationalism*, Bloomington (Ind.) 1978.
Soucy, R., *Fascism in France. The Case of Maurice Barrès*, Berkeley (Calif.) 1972.
Stern, F., *The Politics of Cultural Despair. A Study in the Rise of the German Ideology*, Berkeley (Calif.) 1961.
Sternhell, Z., 'Paul Déroulède and the Origins of Modern French Nationalism', in: *Journal of Contemporary History* 6 (1971), pp. 46–70.
Stoakes, G., *Hitler and the Quest for World Domination*, Leamington Spa 1986.
Thaden, E. C. (ed.), *Russification in the Baltic Provinces and Finland, 1855–1914*, Princeton (NJ) 1981.
Tombs, R. (ed.), *Nationhood and Nationalism in France: From Boulangism to the Great War, 1889–1918*, London 1991.
Umegaki, M., *After the Restoration. The Beginnings of Japan's Modern State*, New York 1988.
Ward, R. E. and D. A. Rustow (eds), *Political Modernization in Japan and Turkey*, Princeton (NJ) 1964.
Webber, G. C., *The Ideology of the British Right 1918–1939*, London 1986.
Weber, E., *Action Française. Royalism and Reaction in Twentieth-Century France*, Stanford (Calif.) 1962.
—— *Peasants into Frenchmen. The Modernization of Rural France, 1870–1914*, Princeton (NJ) 1976.
Wehler, H.-U., *The German Empire 1871–1918*, Leamington Spa 1985.
Wertheimer, M. S., *The Pan-German League 1890–1914* (1924), repr. New York 1971.

Westney, D. E., *Imitation and Innovation. The Transfer of Western Organizational Patterns to Meiji Japan*, Cambridge (Mass.) 1988.
Woolf, S. J. (ed.), *Fascism in Europe*, London 1981.
Yoshino, K., *Cultural Nationalism in Contemporary Japan*, London 1992.
Zürcher, E. J., *Turkey. A Modern History*, London 1993.

III Risorgimento Nationalism in Europe

Anderson, E. N., *Nationalism and the Cultural Crisis in Prussia, 1806–1815* (1939), repr. New York 1976.
Armstrong, J. A., *Nations before Nationalism*, Chapel Hill (NC) 1982.
Austensen, R. A., 'Austria and the "Struggle for Supremacy in Germany", 1848–1864', in: *Journal of Modern History* 52 (1980), pp. 195–225.
Avineri, S., *The Social and Political Thought of Karl Marx*, Cambridge 1980.
Barnard, F. M., *Herder's Social and Political Thought: From Enlightenment to Nationalism*, Oxford 1965.
Beales, D., *The Risorgimento and the Unification of Italy*, 2nd ed., London 1981.
Beckett, J. C., *The Making of Modern Ireland, 1603–1923*, London 1966.
Bell, W. and W. E. Freeman (eds), *Ethnicity and Nation-Building. Comparative, International, and Historical Perspectives*, Beverly Hills (Calif.) 1974.
Bendix, R., *Nation Building and Citizenship. Studies of Our Changing Social Order*, Berkeley (Calif.) 1977.
—— 'Why Nationalism? Relative Backwardness and Intellectual Mobilization', in: *Zeitschrift für Soziologie* 8 (1979), pp. 6–13.
Benner, E. L., 'Marx and Engels on Nationalism and National Identity: A Reappraisal', in: *Millenium. Journal of International Studies* 17 (1988), pp. 1–23.
Berlin, I., *Vico and Herder. Two Studies in the History of Ideas*, London 1976.
Blanning, T. C. W., *The French Revolution in Germany. Occupation and Resistance in the Rhineland 1792–1802*, Oxford 1983.
Boyce, D. G., *Nationalism in Ireland*, London 1982.
Bradley, J. F., *Czech Nationalism in the Nineteenth Century*, Boulder (Col.) 1984.
Bradshaw, B., 'Nationalism and Historical Scholarship in Modern Ireland', in: *Irish Historical Studies* 26 (1989), pp. 329–51.
Brock, P., *The Slovak National Awakening. An Essay in the Intellectual History of East Central Europe*, Toronto 1976.
Clark S. and J. S. Donnelly (eds), *Irish Peasants: Violence and Political Unrest 1780–1914*, Manchester 1983.
Cohler, A. M., *Rousseau and Nationalism*, New York 1970.
Connor, W., 'Nation-Building or Nation-Destroying', in: *World Politics* 24 (1972), pp. 319–55.
Cowie, L. and R. Wolfson (eds), *Years of Nationalism. European History 1815–1890*, London 1985.
Cronin, S., *Irish Nationalism. A History of its Roots and Ideology*, Dublin 1980.
Cummins, I., *Marx, Engels and National Movements*, London 1980.
Davis, H. B., *Towards a Marxist Theory of Nationalism*, London 1978.
Deletant, D. and H. Hanak (eds), *Historians as Nation Builders. Central and South-East Europe*, London 1988.
Derry, T. K., *A History of Modern Norway 1814–1972*, Oxford 1973.
Eddy, J. and D. Schreuder (eds), *The Rise of Colonial Nationalism. Australia, New Zealand, Canada and South Africa First Assert their Nationalities, 1880–1914*, Sydney 1988.

Ergang, R. R., *Herder and the Foundations of German Nationalism*, New York 1931.
Forsyth, M., *Reason and Revolution. The Political Thought of the Abbé Sieyès*, Leicester 1987.
Gella, A. (ed.), *The Intelligentsia and the Intellectuals*, Beverly Hills (Calif.) 1976.
Grew, R., *A Sterner Plan for Italian Unity. The Italian National Society in the Risorgimento*, Princeton (NJ) 1963.
Hamerow, T. S., *Restoration, Revolution, Reaction. Economics and Politics in Germany, 1815–1871*, Princeton (NJ) 1972.
Hearder, H., *Italy in the Age of the Risorgimento 1790–1870*, London 1983.
Hobsbawm, E. J., *The Age of Revolution. Europe 1789–1848*, 4th ed., London 1984.
—— and T. Ranger (eds), *The Invention of Tradition*, Cambridge 1983.
Holt, E., *Risorgimento. The Making of Italy 1815–1870*, London 1970.
Hroch, M., *Social Preconditions of National Revival in Europe. A Comparative Analysis of the Social Composition of Patriotic Groups among Smaller European Nations*, Cambridge 1985.
Hutchinson, J., *The Dynamics of Cultural Nationalism. The Gaelic Revival and the Creation of the Irish Nation State*, London 1987.
Isaacs, H. R., *Idols of the Tribe. Group Identity and Political Change*, New York 1975.
Jászi, O., *The Dissolution of the Habsburg Monarchy* (1929), repr. London 1971.
Kann, R. A., *A History of the Habsburg Empire 1526–1918*, Berkeley (Calif.) 1974.
Karpat, K. H., *An Inquiry into the Social Foundations of Nationalism in the Ottoman State. From Social Estates to Classes, from Millets to Nations*, Princeton (NJ) 1973.
Katzenstein, P. J., *Disjoined Partners. Austria and Germany since 1815*, Berkeley (Calif.) 1976.
Kee, R., *The Green Flag. A History of Irish Nationalism*, London 1972.
Kellogg, F., 'The Structure of Romanian Nationalism', in: *Canadian Review of Studies in Nationalism* 11 (1984), pp. 21–50.
Kohn, H., 'Romanticism and the Rise of Nationalism', in: *Review of Politics* 12 (1950), pp. 443–72.
Lee, J. J., *Ireland 1912–1985. Politics and Society*, Cambridge 1989.
Leslie, R. F., *The History of Poland since 1863*, Cambridge 1980.
McCaffrey, L. J., *The Irish Question 1800–1922*, Lexington (Ken.) 1968.
Mackenzie, D., *The Serbs and Russian Pan-Slavism, 1875–1878*, Ithaca (NY) 1967.
Mack Smith, D., *Cavour*, New York 1985.
—— *Victor Emanuel, Cavour and the Risorgimento*, London 1971.
Mandle, W. F., *The Gaelic Athletic Association and Irish Nationalist Politics 1884–1924*, London 1987.
Marcu, E. D., *Sixteenth-Century Nationalism*, New York 1976.
Mews, S. (ed.), *Religion and National Identity*, Oxford 1982.
Namier, L., *1848: The Revolution of the Intellectuals*, 6th ed., Oxford 1971.
Niederhauser, E., *The Rise of Nationality in Eastern Europe*, Budapest 1982.
O'Day, A. (ed.), *Reactions to Irish Nationalism*, London 1987.
Pech, S. Z., *The Czech Revolution of 1848*, Chapel Hill (NC) 1969.
Petrovich, M. B., *The Emergence of Russian Pan-Slavism, 1856–70*, New York 1956.
Pflanze, O., *Bismarck and the Development of Germany. The Period of Unification, 1815–1871*, Princeton (NJ) 1963.
Philpin, C. H. E. (ed.), *Nationalism and Popular Protest in Ireland*, Cambridge 1987.

Plakans, A., 'Peasants, Intellectuals, and Nationalism in the Russian Baltic Provinces, 1820–90', in: *Journal of Modern History* 46 (1974), pp. 445–75.
Puntila, L. A., *The Political History of Finland 1809–1966*, London 1975.
Reiterer, A. F., 'Leader and Movement. Charismatic Personality, the Armed Forces, and Party as Instruments of Nation-Building', in: *Canadian Review of Studies in Nationalism* 11 (1984), pp. 51–62.
Smith, D. E. (ed.), *Religion and Political Modernization*, New Haven (Conn.) 1974.
Snyder, L. L., *Macro-Nationalism. A History of the Pan-Movements*, Westport (Conn.) 1984.
Sugar, P. F. and I. J. Lederer (eds), *Nationalism in Eastern Europe*, London 1969.
Sussex, R. and J. C. Eade (eds), *Culture and Nationalism in Nineteenth-Century Eastern Europe*, Columbus (Ohio) 1984.
Thomas, R. H., *Liberalism, Nationalism and the German Intellectuals 1822–1847. An Analysis of the Academic and Scientific Conferences of the Period* (1951), repr. Westport (Conn.) 1975.
Wandycz, P. S., *The Lands of Partitioned Poland, 1795–1918*, London 1974.
Wilson, F. A., *Folklore and Nationalism in Modern Finland*, Bloomington (Ind.) 1976.
Woodhouse, C. M., *Modern Greece. A Short History*, London 1968.
Woolf, S. J., *A History of Italy 1700–1860. The Social Constraints of Political Change*, London 1979.
Zakynthinos, D. A., *The Making of Modern Greece. From Byzantium to Independence*, Oxford 1976.

IV The Nation-State as a Form of Political Organization

Akzin, B., *State and Nation*, London 1964.
Archer, J., 'But is it Australian Nationalism?', in: *The Australian Journal of Politics and History* 36 (1990), pp. 84–93.
Attalides, M. A., *Cyprus. Nationalism and International Politics*, Edinburgh 1979.
Avineri, S., *The Making of Modern Zionism. The Intellectual Origins of the Jewish State*, London 1981.
Bitsios, D. S., *Cyprus. The Vulnerable Republic*, Thessaloniki 1975.
Bobango, G. J., *The Emergence of the Romanian National State*, Boulder (Col.) 1979.
Cobban, A., *The Nation State and National Self-Determination*, London 1969.
Curran, J. M., *The Birth of the Irish Free State 1921–1923*, University (Alab.) 1980.
Dakin, D., *The Unification of Greece 1770–1923*, London 1972.
Eyck, F., *The Frankfurt Parliament, 1848–1849*, London 1968.
Flapan, S., *The Birth of Israel. Myths and Realities*, London 1987.
Forsyth, M. (ed.), *Federalism and Nationalism*, Leicester 1989.
George, D., 'The Right of National Self-Determination', in: *History of European Ideas* 16 (1993), pp. 507–13.
Griffiths, P., *Empire to Commonwealth*, London 1969.
Gunter, M. M., *The Kurds in Turkey: A Political Dilemma*, Boulder (Col.) 1990.
Haas, E. B., *Beyond the Nation-State. Functionalism and International Organization*, Stanford (Calif.) 1964.
Hagen, W. W., *Germans, Poles and Jews. The Nationality Conflict in the Prussian East, 1772–1914*, London 1980.
Hamerow, T. S., *The Birth of a New Europe. State and Society in the Nineteenth Century*, London 1983.

Hinsley, F. H., *Nationalism and the International System*, London 1973.

Jelavich, B., *Russia and the Formation of the Romanian National State, 1821–1878*, Cambridge 1984.

—— *Modern Austria. Empire and Republic, 1815–1986*, Cambridge 1987.

Jelavich, C., *Tsarist Russia and Balkan Nationalism. Russian Influence in the Internal Affairs of Bulgaria and Serbia, 1879–1886*, Berkeley (Calif.) 1959.

—— and B. Jelavich, *The Establishment of the Balkan National States, 1804–1920*, London 1977.

Kalvoda, J., *The Genesis of Czechoslovakia*, Boulder (Col.) 1986.

Kann, R. A., *The Multinational Empire. Nationalism and National Reform in the Habsburg Monarchy, 1848–1918* (1950), 2 vols, repr. New York 1977.

Kaye, H. J. (ed.), *History, Classes and Nation-States. Selected Writings of Victor Kiernan*, Oxford 1988.

Kent, M. (ed.), *The Great Powers and the End of the Ottoman Empire*, London 1984.

Kohn, H., *Prelude to Nation-States. The French and German Experience, 1789–1815*, Princeton (NJ) 1967.

Komarnicki, T., *Rebirth of the Polish Republic. A Study in the Diplomatic History of Europe, 1914–1920*, London 1957.

Macartney, C. A., *National States and National Minorities*, London 1934.

—— *The Habsburg Empire 1790–1918*, London 1968.

Mack Smith, D., *Italy. A Modern History*, Ann Arbor (Mich.) 1969.

—— (ed.), *The Making of Italy 1796–1870*, 2nd ed., London 1978.

Mann, M. (ed.), *The Rise and Decline of the Nation State*, Oxford 1990.

Mosse, W. E., *The European Powers and the German Question 1848–1871 with Special Reference to England and Russia*, Cambridge 1958.

Orton, L. D., *The Prague Slav Congress of 1848*, New York 1978.

Pearson, R., *National Minorities in Eastern Europe 1848–1945*, London 1985.

Poggi, G., *The Development of the Modern State*, London 1978.

Robins, P., 'The Overlord State: Turkish Policy and the Kurdish Issue', in: *International Affairs* 69 (1993), pp. 657–76.

Schmid, C. L., *Conflict and Consensus in Switzerland*, Berkeley (Calif.) 1981.

Schroeder, P. W., 'The 19th-Century International System: Changes in the Structure', in: *World Politics* 39 (1986), pp. 1–26.

Sharp, A., 'Britain and the Protection of Minorities at the Paris Peace Conference, 1919', in: A. C. Hepburn (ed.), *Minorities in History*, London 1978, pp. 170–88.

Silverman, D. P., *Reluctant Union. Alsace-Lorraine and Imperial Germany 1871–1918*, University Park (Penn.) 1972.

Steinberg, J., *Why Switzerland?*, Cambridge 1976.

Suval, S., *The Anschluss Question in the Weimar Era. A Study of Nationalism in Germany and Austria, 1918–1932*, London 1974.

Tilly, C. (ed.), *The Formation of National States in Western Europe*, Princeton (NJ) 1975.

Tivey, L. J. (ed.), *The Nation-State. The Formation of Modern Politics*, Oxford 1981.

White, R., *Inventing Australia: Images and Identity 1688–1980*, Sydney 1981.

V The Renaissance of Nationalism

I Nationalism and the Nation in Post-War Europe

Barclay, G. S. J., *Twentieth-Century Nationalism*, London 1971.
Beyme, K., 'National Consciousness and Nationalism: The Case of the Two Germanies', in: *Canadian Review of Studies in Nationalism* 13 (1986), pp. 227–48.
Breuilly, J. (ed.), *The State of Germany. The National Idea in the Making, Unmaking and Remaking of a Modern Nation-State*, London 1992.
Burgess, M., *Federalism and European Union: Political Ideas, Influences and Strategies in the European Community 1972–1987*, London 1989.
Friedrich, C. J., *Europe: An Emergent Nation?*, New York 1969.
Glaessner, G.-J. and I. Wallace (eds), *The German Revolution of 1989. Causes and Consequences*, London 1992.
Grosser, D. (ed.), *German Unification: The Unexpected Challenge*, Oxford 1992.
Hughes, E., *Culture and Politics in Northern Ireland 1960–1990*, Buckingham 1991.
Keens-Soper, M., 'The Liberal State and Nationalism in Post-War Europe', in: *History of European Ideas* 10 (1989), pp. 689–703.
Lipgens, W., *A History of European Integration*, Oxford 1982.
Merritt, R. L. and B. M. Russett (eds), *From National Development to Global Community. Essays in Honor of Karl W. Deutsch*, Winchester (Ma.) 1981.
Milward, A. S., *The European Rescue of the Nation-State*, London 1992.
Pryce, R. (ed.), *The Dynamics of European Union*, London 1987.
Rougemont, D. de, *The Meaning of Europe*, London 1965.
Sathyamurthy, T. V., *Nationalism in the Contemporary World: Political and Sociological Perspectives*, London 1983.
Schweigler, G., *National Consciousness in Divided Germany*, Farnborough 1975.
Stirk, P. M. R. (ed.), *European Unity in Context. The Interwar Period*, London 1989.
Tiryakian, E. A. and R. Rogowski (eds), *New Nationalism of the Developed West: Towards Explanation*, Boston 1985.
Tudjman, F., *Nationalism in Contemporary Europe*, New York 1981.
Twitchett, C. and J. Kenneth (eds), *Building Europe. Britain's Partners in the EEC*, London 1981.
Wallace, W., *The Transformation of Western Europe*, London 1990.
Wallach, H. G. P. and R. A. Francisco, *United Germany: the Past, Politics, Prospects*, London 1992.
Young, J. W., *Britain, France and the Unity of Europe 1945–1951*, Leicester 1984.

2 Regionalism in Western Europe

Bogdanor, V., *Devolution*, Oxford 1979.
Brand, J., *The National Movement in Scotland*, London 1978.
Cashmore, E. E., *United Kingdom? Class, Race and Gender since the War*, London 1989.
Collins, R., *The Basques*, Oxford 1986.
Davies, D. H., *The Welsh Nationalist Party, 1925–1945: A Call to Nationhood*, Cardiff 1983.
Esman, M. (ed.), *Ethnic Conflict in the Western World*, Ithaca (NY) 1977.
Foster, C. (ed.), *Nations without a State. Ethnic Minorities in Western Europe*, New York 1980.

Goulbourne, H., *Ethnicity and Nationalism in Post-Imperial Britain*, Cambridge 1991.
Gourevitch, P. A., *Paris and the Provinces. The Politics of Local Government Reform in France*, London 1980.
Hanham, H. J., *Scottish Nationalism*, London 1969.
Harvie, C., *Scotland and Nationalism. Scottish Society and Politics, 1707–1994*, 2nd ed., London 1994.
Heiberg, M., *The Making of the Basque Nation*, Cambridge 1989.
Keating, M., *State and Regional Nationalism. Territorial Politics and the European State*, Hemel Hempstead 1988.
Levy, R., *Scottish Nationalism at the Crossroads*, Edinburgh 1990.
Link, W. and W. J. Feld (eds), *The New Nationalism*, New York 1979.
MacCormick, N. (ed.), *The Scottish Debate. Essays on Scottish Nationalism*, Oxford 1970.
McMillan, J. F., *Twentieth-Century France. Politics and Society 1898–1991*, London 1992.
Mercer, J., *Scotland: The Devolution of Power*, London 1978.
Mingione, E., 'Italy: The Resurgence of Regionalism', in: *International Affairs* 69 (1993), pp. 305–18.
Morgan, K. O., *Rebirth of a Nation. Wales 1880–1980*, Oxford 1981.
Morgan, R. (ed.), *Regionalism in European Politics*, London 1986.
Nairn, T., *The Break-Up of Britain. Crisis and Neo-Nationalism*, London 1977.
'Nationalism and Separatism', in: *Journal of Contemporary History* 6 (1971), pp. 1–196.
O'Halloran, C., *Partition and the Limits of Irish Nationalism. An Ideology under Stress*, Dublin 1987.
Payne, S. G., *Basque Nationalism*, Reno 1975.
Reinharz, J. and G. L. Mosse (eds), *The Impact of Western Nationalisms*, London 1992.
Samuel, R. (ed.), *Patriotism: The Making and Unmaking of British National Identity*, 3 vols, London 1989.
Sharpe, L. J., 'Devolution and Celtic Nationalism in the United Kingdom', in: *West European Politics* 8 (1985), pp. 82–100.
Smith, A. D., *The Ethnic Revival in the Modern World*, Cambridge 1981.
Snyder, L. L., *Global Mini-Nationalisms: Autonomy or Independence*, Westport (Conn.) 1982.
—— *The New Nationalism*, Ithaca (NY) 1968.
Sullivan, J. L., *ETA and Basque Nationalism. The Fight for Euskadi 1890–1986*, London 1988.
Tägil, S. (ed.), *Regions in Upheaval*, Stockholm 1984.
Walker, N. J. and R. M. Worcester, 'Nationalism in Great Britain', in: *Canadian Review of Studies in Nationalism* 13 (1986), pp. 249–69.
Watson, M. (ed.), *Contemporary Minority Nationalism*, London 1990 (repr. 1992).
Webb, K., *The Growth of Nationalism in Scotland*, Harmondsworth 1977.
Williams, C. H. (ed.), *National Separatism*, London 1982.
Williams, G., *Religion, Language and Nationality in Wales*, Cardiff 1979.
Zariski, R., *Italy. The Politics of Uneven Development*, Hinsdale 1972.

3 Nationalism after Communism in Eastern Europe

Allworth, E., *The Nationality Question in Soviet Central Asia*, New York 1973.
Banac, I., *The National Question in Yugoslavia. Origins, History, Politics*, London 1984.

Bertsch, G. K., *Nation-Building in Yugoslavia. A Study of Political Integration and Attitudinal Consensus*, London 1971.

Bon, A. and R. van Voren (eds), *Nationalism in the USSR. Problems of Nationalities*, Amsterdam 1989.

Bremmer, I. and R. Taras (eds), *Nations and Politics in the Soviet Successor States*, Cambridge 1993.

Carter, S. K., *Russian Nationalism. Yesterday, Today, Tomorrow*, London 1990.

Critchlow, J., *Nationalism in Uzbekistan*, Boulder (Col.) 1991.

Djordjevic, D. (ed.), *The Creation of Yugoslavia 1914–1918*, Santa Barbara (Calif.) 1980.

Dunlop, J. B., *The Faces of Contemporary Russian Nationalism*, Princeton (NJ) 1983.

Fisher, J. C., *Yugoslavia: A Multinational State*, San Francisco 1966.

Gilberg, T., *Nationalism and Communism in Romania. The Rise and Fall of Ceausescu's Personal Dictatorship*, Boulder (Col.) 1990.

Gleason, G., *Federalism and Nationalism. The Struggle for Republican Rights in the USSR*, Boulder (Col.) 1990.

Glenny, M., *Rebirth of History: Eastern Europe in the Age of Democracy*, Harmondsworth 1992.

Huttenbach, H. H. (ed.), *Soviet Nationalities Policy. Ruling Ethnic Groups in the USSR*, London 1990.

Joncic, K., *Nationalities in Yugoslavia*, Belgrade 1982.

King, R. R., *Minorities under Communism. Nationalities as a Source of Tension among Balkan Communist States*, Cambridge (Mass.) 1973.

Lapidus, G. et al. (eds), *From Union to Commonwealth. Nationalism and Separatism in the Soviet Republics*, Cambridge 1992.

Pavlowitch, S. K., *The Improbable Survivor. Yugoslavia and its Problems 1918–1988*, London 1988.

Pipes, R., *The Formation of the Soviet Union. Communism and Nationalism 1917–1923*, Cambridge (Mass.) 1954.

Ramet, S. P., *Nationalism and Federalism in Yugoslavia, 1962–1991*, 2nd ed., Bloomington (Ind.) 1992.

—— (ed.), *Religion and Nationalism in Soviet and East European Politics*, Durham (NC) 1984.

—— (ed.), *Yugoslavia in the 1980s*, Boulder (Col.) 1985.

Rusinow, D. J., *The Yugoslav Experiment, 1948–1974*, London 1977.

Singleton, F. B., *Twentieth-Century Yugoslavia*, London 1976.

Skalnik Leff, C., *National Conflict in Czechoslovakia: The Making and Remaking of a State, 1918–1987*, Princeton (NJ) 1988.

Smith, G., *The Nationalities Question in the Soviet Union*, London 1991.

Szporluk, R., *Communism and Nationalism: Karl Marx versus Friedrich List*, Oxford 1989.

Vukadinovic, R., *The Break-Up of Yugoslavia: Threats and Challenges*, The Hague 1992.

4 Nationalism in the Third World

Ahmed, I., *Nationalities in South Asia*, Oxford 1993.

Behbehani, H. S. H., *The Soviet Union and Arab Nationalism, 1917–1966*, London 1986.

Boahen, A. A., *African Perspectives on Colonialism*, London 1987.

Cain, P. J., *British Imperialism. Crisis and Deconstruction 1914–1990*, London 1993.

Carter, G. (ed.), *National Unity and Regionalism in Eight African States*, Ithaca (NY) 1966.

Chatterjee, P., *Nationalist Thought and the Colonial World. A Derivative Discourse?*, London 1986.

Coleman, J. S., 'Tradition and Nationalism in Africa', in: M. L. Kilson (ed.), *New States in the Modern World*, Cambridge (Mass.) 1975, pp. 3–36.

—— *Nigeria. Background to Nationalism*, Berkeley (Calif.) 1963.

Dahm, B., *History of Indonesia in the Twentieth Century*, New York 1971.

Darwin, J., *The End of the British Empire. The Historical Debate*, Oxford 1991.

Duri, A. A., *The Historical Formation of the Arab Nation. A Study in Identity and Consciousness*, London 1987.

Emerson, R., *From Empire to Nation. The Rise to Self-Assertion of Asian and African Peoples*, Cambridge (Mass.) 1962.

Etzel Pearcy, G. and E. A. Stoneman, *A Handbook of New Nations*, New York 1968.

Fishman, J. A. (ed.), *Language Problems in Developing Countries*, New York 1968.

Geiss, I., *The Pan-African Movement*, London 1974.

Gulliver, P. H. (ed.), *Tradition and Transition in East Africa*, London 1969.

Hodgkin, T. L., *Nationalism in Colonial Africa*, 5th ed., London 1965.

Kang, T. S. (ed.)., *Nationalism and the Crises of Ethnic Minorities in Asia*, Westport (Conn.) 1979.

Kedourie, E. (ed.), *Nationalism in Asia and Africa*, London 1971.

Kimble, D., *A Political History of Ghana. The Rise of Gold Coast Nationalism, 1850–1928*, Oxford 1963.

Langley, J. A., *Pan-Africanism and Nationalism in West Africa 1900–1945. A Study in Ideology and Social Classes*, Oxford 1973.

Legum, C., *Pan-Africanism. A Short Political Guide*, London 1962.

Lewis, J. M. (ed.), *Nationalism and Self-Determination in the Horn of Africa*, London 1983.

Masur, G., *Nationalism in Latin America. Diversity and Unity*, London 1966.

Mazrui, A. A., *The African Condition. A Political Diagnosis*, London 1980.

—— and M. Tidy, *Nationalism and New States in Africa*, London 1984.

Morris-Jones, W. H. and G. Fischer (eds), *Decolonisation and After. The British and French Experience*, London 1980.

Neuberger, B., 'State and Nation in African Thought', in: *Journal of African Studies* 4 (1977), pp. 198–205.

—— 'The Western Nation-State in African Perceptions of Nation-Building', in: *Asian and African Studies* 11 (1976), pp. 241–61.

Piscatori, J. P., *Islam in a World of Nation-States*, Cambridge 1986.

Rotberg, R. J., *The Rise of Nationalism in Central Africa. The Making of Malawi and Zambia 1873–1964*, Cambridge (Mass.) 1965.

Rothermund, D., *The Phases of Indian Nationalism and Other Essays*, Bombay 1970.

Saul, J., *The State and Revolution in East Africa*, London 1979.

Schwarz, F. A. O., *Nigeria, the Tribes, the Nation, or the Race. The Politics of Independence*, Cambridge (Mass.) 1965.

Seal, A., *The Emergence of Indian Nationalism*, Cambridge 1968.

Sharabi, H., *Nationalism and Revolution in the Arab World*, Princeton (NJ) 1966.

Sisson, R. and S. Wolpert (eds), *Congress and Indian Nationalism. The Pre-Independence Phase*, Berkeley (Calif.) 1988.

Smith, A. D., *State and Nation in the Third World. The Western State and African Nationalism*, New York 1983.

Syme, R., *Colonial Elites*, Oxford 1970.
Tibi, B., *Arab Nationalism. A Critical Enquiry*, New York 1981.
Whitaker, A. P. and D. C. Jordan, *Nationalism in Contemporary Latin America*,
    New York 1966.
Wilson, H. S. (ed.), *The Origins of West African Nationalism*, London 1969.
—— *African Decolonization*, London 1993.

Index